THE
PRAYER
OF
JESUS

THE
PRAYER
OF
JESUS

*The Promise and Power of Living
in the Lord's Prayer*

KEN HEMPHILL

BROADMAN
&HOLMAN
PUBLISHERS

Nashville, Tennesse

0-8054-2567-5

Published by Broadman & Holman Publishers,
Nashville, Tennessee

Dewey Decimal Classification: 226.9
Subject Heading: PRAYER
Library of Congress Card Catalog Number: 2001046482

Unless otherwise stated, all Scripture used is from the NASB, the New American Standard Bible, © the Lockman Foundation, 1960, 1962, 1963, 1968, 1971, 1972, 1973, 1975, 1977, 1995; used by permission. Other versions used include the NIV, the Holy Bible, New International Version, copyright © 1973, 1978, 1984 by International Bible Society.

Library of Congress Cataloging-in-Publication Data
Hemphill, Kenneth S., 1948–
      The prayer of Jesus: the promise and power of living in the Lord's prayer / Kenneth S. Hemphill.
          p. cm.
      ISBN 0-8054-2567-5
      1. Lord's Prayer. I. Title.
BV230 .H46 2001
226.9'606—dc21

2001046482

2 3 4 5 6 7 8 9 10 01 02 03 04 05

DEDICATION

It is an honor to dedicate this book to my life's
companion, Paula Moore Hemphill.
She is the epitome of a loving wife
and a model mother.
She is my prayer partner and one of the
greatest prayer warriors I know.

ACKNOWLEDGMENTS

This book has been a labor of love and a community effort. It is a moving and humbling experience to attempt to elaborate on the model prayer given by our Lord. Throughout this writing assignment, I have felt a certain sense of divine compulsion and guidance.

I owe a tremendous debt of gratitude to my wife, Paula, who models "praying without ceasing." She has been a sounding board throughout this project. All those who know Paula will understand why this particular book is dedicated to her. I am greatly indebted to my three daughters, Kristina, Rachael, and Katie. Watching them grow in their conversation with the Father has provided many of the illustrations in this book.

One of the advantages of serving as president of one of the world's great seminaries is that I am surrounded by one of the finest faculties ever assembled. No one has been more helpful on this project than Paul Wolfe, one of our fine New Testament scholars. I am indebted to him for his many insights freely shared. My administrative assistant, Barbara Walker, has worked closely with me to provide a readable first draft.

It has been a pleasure to work with my good friends at Broadman & Holman. I have been greatly encouraged by their enthusiasm for this project. In particular, Lawrence Kimbrough has skillfully and patiently reorganized—and at times rewritten—my first draft to make it much more readable.

I give thanks to God for the privilege of contributing this small volume on prayer. I pray that it will add in some way to the large number of wonderful books already available to the Christian who desires to live a "kingdom-focused" life. I sincerely believe that following Jesus' pattern for praying could revolutionize our families, our churches, our communities, and our world.

CONTENTS

Acknowledgments   vi

Introduction: An Answer to Prayer   1

Chapter 1: Till You're Blue in the Face
Three Reasons Prayer Doesn't Seem to Work   7

Chapter 2: God and the Family Tree
Three Realities from the Prayer of Jesus   25

Chapter 3: Anytime, Anywhere
Three Responsibilities from the Prayer of Jesus   43

Chapter 4: I've Got You Covered
Three Requests from the Prayer of Jesus   63

Chapter 5: Feel the Power
Three Reminders from the Prayer of Jesus   83

Epilogue: Prayer Suggestions   95

Appendix: The Names of God   101

Endnotes   104

Our Father who art in heaven,
Hallowed be Thy name.
Thy kingdom come.
Thy will be done,
On earth as it is in heaven.
Give us this day our daily bread.
And forgive us our debts,
as we also have forgiven our debtors.
And do not lead us into temptation,
but deliver us from evil.
For Thine is the kingdom, and the power,
and the glory, forever. Amen.
Matthew 6: 9–13

INTRODUCTION

AN ANSWER TO PRAYER

Several years ago, the investment firm E. F. Hutton aired a series of commercials that shared a common thread. Amid the buzz of spectators at a tennis match, diners at an exclusive restaurant, or passengers near the luggage claim rack at the airport, someone would whisper, "My broker is E. F. Hutton, and E. F. Hutton says . . ." At that, everyone in the room would stop what they were doing, craning their necks or cupping their ears as the announcer's voice would matter-of-factly declare: "When E. F. Hutton talks, people listen."

The implication is obvious. Serious investors who want to maximize their earnings potential will listen with diligent attention and eagerness to their favorite financial experts. Those who dream of improving their skills at everything from making putts to puttering in the garden never tire of hearing a Tiger Woods or Martha Stewart explain the subtle nuances of their craft.

But how important are solid portfolios, lush azaleas, or a masterful short game when life gets hard and the usual answers can't dull the pain, when the suffering is serious and recreation no longer provides a viable escape. That's when all kinds of people with all kinds of interests find themselves wanting one thing more than just about any other. They want to know how to pray.

"I know," you might say, "but I've tried prayer, and it just doesn't work for me."

Have you ever said those words? Maybe they're not the kind of words you speak out loud, but they've probably run through your mind at some point in your life.

Truth is, it's a fair statement. And even those of us who profoundly disagree with the conclusion must honestly confess that it at least raises some good questions:

- What *is* prayer?
- Why *doesn't* it always work the way we think it should?
- And who *knows* the answers to questions like these anyway?

MY OWN STRUGGLE

I'll be the first to admit it: I've struggled over the years to have a consistent prayer life. Yes. Me. I mean, you'd think if anyone would have a handle on prayer, it would be a preacher turned seminary president.

But I can tell you this, and I imagine you can say the same thing: *Desire* hasn't been the problem. I have wanted to be close to God in prayer more than just about anything. But I could never seem to find that . . . something . . . that enabled me to find my way through the fog of an ineffective prayer life, to know that I was honestly communicating with my Creator and Father in a way that was pleasing to Him.

Of course, I've long known the biblical truths about prayer. I've taught and preached on the promises of God.

I've quoted with great conviction those luminaries from the past who declared their confidence in prayer. But I have long had a passion to experience it myself on a daily, ongoing basis.

Over the years I have tried numerous strategies to improve my own prayer life and to be able to communicate to others how they, too, could approach God effectively. And some of those ideas have helped. But a few years ago I made a profound discovery—perhaps I should more rightly say that God opened my mind to something absolutely life-changing I had been missing before—that has transformed my own prayer life and energized my daily walk with the Lord.

As a result I have gained new confidence and consistency in prayer. I have witnessed God doing incredible things in my own heart and in my own world. I have found that prayer has a purpose that goes far beyond answers, prayer lists, and quiet time in the morning.

I have seen what prayer can do and I have seen it work. But I'm certainly not the first one to learn this secret to effective praying. For that, you'd have to go back nearly two thousand years, sit down at the feet of the Master with His first-century followers, and see what Jesus Christ had to say about prayer.

Teach Us to Pray

That small group of disciples must have asked Him many questions over the course of His three years on earth.

But the most significant request they ever made of Him was this:

> It happened that while Jesus was praying in a certain place, after He had finished, one of His disciples said to Him, "Lord, teach us to pray just as John also taught his disciples." (Luke 11:1)

Bear in mind that this request came from men who had seen Jesus heal the terminally sick, cast out legions of demons, and exercise amazing authority over nature. They had sensed firsthand the excitement of the crowds who flocked to hear Him teach. They had experienced all the hubbub of being part of an exhilarating cause attracting wide attention.

Yet none of the disciples—as far as we know—asked Jesus to school them in any of the more visible ministry abilities, like personal counseling, public speaking, or miracle working.

All they wanted to know was this: *How do you pray like that?*

Somehow from observing Jesus, they knew that prayer—or at least something that happened to Him in the process of prayer—was the key that gave Him the strength to do all the other miraculous things He did. Jesus knew a level of intimacy with His heavenly Father that did much more than transform prayer from ritual into privilege, but from privilege into raw, living, breathing power. He knew what prayer was, and His prayer connected!

Now these men who were asking Jesus for instructions weren't beginners when it came to prayer. They had been praying all their lives. Their Jewish heritage required them to be disciplined and consistent in the practice of prayer all the way back to their early childhood. At the beginning and ending of each day, for as long as they could remember, they had quoted the Shema, the Jewish confession of faith taken from Deuteronomy 6:4–5, along with other prayers and benedictions. They had also followed the custom of praying three times a day at fixed hours as well as before and after every meal. In fact, some historians say that the average Jew during the time of Jesus prayed an average of three to four hours a day. Put it all together, multiply by their ages, and you could fill the Jordan River with the number of prayers they had showered toward heaven in their lifetimes.

I don't know about you, but I'm not at this level. If *these* men needed help with prayer, I know I need to hear what Jesus had to say.

Obviously, their request of Jesus wasn't about amounts and quantities, schedules and timetables. They had those kinds of details down to a science. Yet they knew something was missing, even with their habitual practice of prayer. They were dying to know what prayer was all about. They craved to experience the intimate communion Jesus had with God. They had seen it in His eyes, in His pace, in His calm. They just had to know.

So He told them. And like most of Jesus' answers, it was simple and straightforward, concise yet comprehensive. We call His answer the Lord's Prayer.

LEARNING TOGETHER

Sadly, Christ's words have become merely common-place—a whispered murmur that speaks in cold black and white what God intended as a way to color our lives with His vivid, personal presence.

So this is not a book that simply *explains* the Lord's Prayer, as others have capably done before. This is a guide to help you use this prayer as a *pattern* throughout your day—an ongoing prayer outline—enabling you to "pray without ceasing" as the Bible teaches, not just in the echoed halls of a Sunday church service.

This book is not to be read and discarded; it is to be read and practiced.

- Do you want to know what prayer is? And how to ensure that it connects?
- Do you want to learn more about God the Father than you have ever known before and more about yourself at the same time?
- Do you want to communicate more effectively with the One who loved you so much that He sent His own Son to die in your place?

I do. So did they. That's what this book is all about.

TILL YOU'RE BLUE IN THE FACE

THREE REASONS PRAYER DOESN'T SEEM TO WORK

Remember the old joke about the guy who angrily brought his new chain saw back to the hardware store for a replacement? He stormed through the door and flung his purchase hard onto the front counter. It lay there, rocking slowly for a moment, bent and beat up, much of the paint chipped off and the teeth at all angles.

"I've been using this thing all day," he sputtered to the first face within shouting range, "and I haven't cut even a handful of firewood!"

The sales clerk, trying hard to remain cooperative, assured the man he'd be glad to take a look at it and do what he could. The saw was a mangled mess, all right. And trying to see if it might start in this condition seemed a foolish waste of time. But not knowing where else to begin, he took a chance and yanked hard one time on the rip cord. Sure enough, after several uncertain seconds of tired gasps and coughs, the motor somehow rattled its way to full throttle.

The red-faced customer suddenly went white, backing two full steps away from the counter in stunned confusion.

"So *that's* what that string was for!"

WHAT'S THE POINT OF PRAYER?

Here's the point: Before concluding that prayer doesn't "work," you need to ask yourself how you've been trying to use it.

- Have you been praying according to the proper guidelines in the manner that the Master himself taught?
- What have you been expecting prayer to do for you? And what would it look like to you if it *were* "working"?
- In fact, is prayer actually supposed to "work" at all? Does it perhaps have a purpose far more significant than the shallow practicality we expect of a gas-powered lawn tool? Would it be asking far too little of prayer—and far too little of God—to demand that it, and He, perform just the way we want them to?

The answers to most of these questions are found in the sixth chapter of Matthew, in the middle of what we call the Sermon on the Mount. This teaching of Jesus, which covers three solid chapters of the Bible, contains instructions that are absolutely basic to understanding what it means to be a follower of Christ. And imbedded among them is a clear pattern of what God says prayer is supposed to be and do—the highest achievements that prayer is designed to fulfill.

This is how prayer works.

> "You, when you pray, go to your inner room, close your door and pray to your Father who is in secret, and your Father who sees what is done in secret will reward you." (Matt. 6:6)

I have frequently heard people despair that their prayer wasn't answered. Perhaps someone they loved was sick, and they prayed asking God for healing. But instead of getting better, the person died. They had asked for one thing, but they had gotten another. Therefore, their prayer didn't "work."

Don't misunderstand me. God does answer prayer. I know it from experience. Besides that, the Scripture is full of instances where God's people prayed and He responded exactly as they had asked.

However, having our requests granted is not the primary goal of prayer. Prayer is not simply the process of giving God our wish list. Many times we ask for things that seem to be what we need, but we later recognize that— had we gotten them—they would have been far from our best interests. God does not exist merely to give us what we want.

Neither is prayer a way to alert God to our needs. As we'll see later in this Bible passage, God knows our needs even better than we do, and He needs no formal reminders about where we are and what we're up against. Prayer is in no way a squeaky wheel designed to manipulate God into remembering us.

One of the most primary purposes of prayer is to spend time in conversation with our Father. And when this is our goal, we can pray at all times *guaranteed* that it will be rewarded.

Will it be answered the way we want it to? Maybe.

But will it be rewarded by bringing us into the Father's presence? Absolutely.

You see, prayer is not about answers. Prayer is about reward.

I'm telling you, this understanding of the purpose of prayer will begin to revolutionize the way you approach God. It will cause you to marvel at the miraculous privilege of being able to engage in intimate conversation with the Creator of the universe. By His own grace and design, He has chosen to become our Father. He has opened the windows of heaven and allowed us to spend hours at a time in His awesome presence. In fact, as we'll continue to see throughout this book, this fellowship is hardly limited to what we usually consider our "prayer time" but is truly a constant, continuous, moment-by-moment relationship with God.

And you can enjoy His reward *every time you pray.*

What Did You Bring Me?

Before I accepted the presidency of Southwestern Seminary, I spent a great deal of time flying across America to lead church growth conferences. I felt all the usual guilt over leaving my family for several days each week. So like many frequent travelers, I got into the habit of always bringing home a small gift for my two girls who were still home at the time.

It happened almost without fail. As soon as my car would enter the driveway, they would run from the house and greet me with the tender address, "Hi, Daddy. What did you bring us?"—their words and their hands coming out simultaneously. They would feel through my pockets, rifle through my briefcase, looking for the gift that they knew was hidden somewhere in my belongings.

After one particularly long and exhausting trip, I arrived home only to be greeted by the same predictable welcome: "What did you bring us, Daddy? What did you bring us?" But for some reason this time, I just wasn't in the mood for giving presents. So instead I gave my girls a short but strong lecture.

I knew they wouldn't be able to relate entirely, but I explained how hard it was to be apart from them and how tired I was every time I came home. I tried to help them imagine what it would feel like for them to be away from their family for days at a time. *Just once,* I expounded, it would mean so much to me if I knew they were simply glad to have Daddy home—not just glad to have a gift.

The following week I returned home after being out of town again, having forgotten about my lecture from the past weekend. As usual, my girls ran to meet me in the driveway—only this time, my youngest, Katie, leaped into my arms, gave me a big hug, and said in the sweetest voice, "I love you, Daddy. I'm so glad you're home."

Ahhhhh. My heart melted within me.

With her next breath, of course, she asked, "Now . . . what did you bring me?"

Well, at least it was a start. She was getting close. But my daughter's behavior made me realize that my own prayers to my heavenly Father often began like that— with little more than requests, requests, requests. I'm sure my words often sounded just like my girls' childish refrain: "What did you bring me, Daddy?"

When I finally comprehended the fact that prayer permitted me to come into the presence of my Father, to express my love for Him, to thank Him for His constant provision and give Him the honor He is due, I discovered a new passion for prayer.

Communicating with Him is reward enough.

And if that is the purpose, there is no such thing as an unanswered prayer.

WHERE PRAYERS GO TO DIE

There *is,* however, such a thing as mistaken prayer— prayer that gets a different kind of reward.

Listen as Jesus describes three of the most common problems we often introduce into our prayer habits.

They are misguided motives that ensure we'll become empty, discouraged, and spiritually out of sorts with God. And apparently these three conditions are universal across the generations because they're just as prevalent now as they must have been in the days when Jesus first spoke these words.

The Phantom Prayer

"When you pray . . ." (Matt. 6:5a)

The first reason prayer doesn't seem to connect people with God is so obvious, I almost hesitate to mention it. In fact, I wouldn't bring it up at all except that it is so pervasive and widespread. You could ask just about any Christian believer if he had been guilty of it at some point in his life, and he would almost certainly confess that he had.

One of the main problems with our prayer is we don't pray. Now this is despite the fact that Jesus speaks repeatedly in these verses with the understood assumption that "when you pray" means there is no question that the follower of Christ will invest himself in prayer. "*When* you pray" says a lot more than "*if* you pray" or "whenever you *feel* like praying." But unfortunately, *"when you pray"* begins at a basic starting point that too many people rarely achieve.

A recent national survey conducted by a mainline Christian denomination indicated that 25 percent of its members admit that they *never* pray. Never! Add this to the number of people who'd be honest enough to tell you that their prayer life is sporadic or dull at best, and it doesn't take a genius to figure out that one glaring reason people are so dissatisfied with their prayer life is simple: They don't pray!

Think of the ridiculous analogies: A football team that never practices. An orchestra that never tunes its instruments. A farmer who never plants any crops. A sales rep who never calls on his clients. An artist who never buys herself any paint. To never do something is the worst way to get any better at it.

But we're too busy, we say. Our schedules stay over-lapped with nonstop activities that keep us about two days and ten minutes behind all the time. And though our demands stressfully require us to keep the plates spinning constantly, somehow the power stays on, the bills get paid, and the dog gets fed whether we pray or not, so . . . we don't. And yet we still expect prayer to work on demand when the wheels come off or the kids get sick, when we resort to pleading with a God we largely ignore during the normal routine of life.

Prayerlessness makes absolutely no sense, yet just about all of us have been guilty of it—and of foolishly putting the blame on God for not answering prayers we never pray.

The Phony Prayer

> "When you pray, you are not to be like the hypocrites; for they love to stand and pray in the synagogues and on the street corners so that they may be seen by men. Truly I say

to you, they have their reward in full."
(Matt. 6:5)

Soon after I dedicated my life to the ministry, I was visiting my dad's church with my wife-to-be. During the service Dad called on me, his "little preacher boy," to deliver the morning prayer. Suddenly feeling myself the focus of attention, I took a deep breath, intoned my best preacher's voice, and wowed the crowd with all the spiritual jargons and theological rhetoric I knew. After I finally reached the "amen" and took my seat, my fiancé, Paula, elbowed me in the side, leaned over, and whispered six sobering words in my ear: "Who were you trying to impress?" I got the message.

But isn't that the way we do it? We preachers may be the worst, using public prayer for everything from reinforcing the points of our sermon to communicating the announcements from the church bulletin board. I shudder to think of how many times I've been complimented for saying a beautiful prayer and took it as a personal accomplishment, how many times I have been more concerned with the way I framed my words than with whether I was honestly communicating with my Father.

Have *you* ever done it—changing both your tone and your vocabulary—so that others could get a feel for your superior spirituality?

Things were no different during the time Jesus was teaching this. To be asked to pray in the synagogue service in first-century Palestine was a mark of distinction. And though prayers were not normally practiced "on the street corners," as the verse says, people who were so inclined probably made a habit of observing their afternoon prayer in a public place—where *they* could be observed as well.

Whatever the case, their driving desire was certainly not to commune with God but to be seen and heard, admired and appreciated. They delighted at the sound of their own voice and the hearty approval of their colleagues.

But Jesus had a succinct response to such showboating—one little phrase that kind of says it all, that takes all the air out of phony praying. He said, "They have their reward."

If you want recognition, good. Take it.

If you want other people's approval, fine. Enjoy it.

If you want us to say you're wonderful, OK. You're wonderful.

Notice the difference between *this* reward and the reward we talked about earlier—the reward for those who prefer the inner room to the public square, who prefer the closed door to the open display—the precious reward of being in the glorious presence of the Father. In the case of the hypocrites, their full reward comes from the crowd, from their friends, in some ways even from themselves—the kind of reward that feels good for a moment but is never enough to satisfy the endless demands of pride. For the humble and pure in heart, however, the reward of prayer comes from God Himself "who sees what is done in secret." And His reward is always enough.

Does this mean we should never pray in public? Of course not. Jesus Himself prayed publicly when He blessed the five loaves and two fish before feeding more than five thousand people with them. The early church in the Book of Acts is shown in public prayer on several occasions.

The problem is not public prayer but praying for effect. Whether in public or in private, we can and should pray with the singular desire of communicating with our Father—and receive the reward of His presence.

The Frivolous Prayer

> "And when you are praying, do not use meaningless repetition as the Gentiles do, for they suppose that they will be heard for their many words." (Matt. 6:7)

To the first-century Greeks and Romans, prayer had both its formal and its magical sides. Since the pagan gods of their religious mythology each controlled some aspect of nature—but couldn't control their own behavior—prayer was the butter that greased the palms of the pantheon. And just in case the gods didn't hear or remember it the first time, these pagan worshipers would often pray the same prayer over and over to make sure they had gotten some heavenly attention, to convince whichever god they wanted that this petition was worth rewarding.

This is different from the idea of *perseverance* in prayer, which Jesus later applauds and encourages. For to these turn-of-the-millennium Gentiles, prayers carried their own magical power. Therefore, it was not merely an issue of repetition but one of repeating a precise formula or incantation that would gain the favor of a god. They thought the more frequently and fervently they spoke these words, the more powerful and effective their prayer became.

Today we would call this a mantra, like the New Age advocate's repeating of a certain phrase or the Muslim repetition of the Shahada.

Jesus called it "meaningless repetition." The actual Greek word for this is *battalogeo*. If you try to pronounce it, you'll notice its similarity to the English term *babbling*. He may have used this term to underline the foolishness of praying in such a singsong manner. On a much earlier day, though, an Old Testament prophet called it a mockery.

First Kings 18 records the spiritual showdown between Elijah, the prophet of God, and 450 pagan prophets of the god Baal. The contest involved two altars—one piled high with wood and sacrifice, the other soaked with (not one, not two, but) twelve huge tubs of water until the runoff puddled up in a trench around the base. The question? Whose god would hear the prayers of his people and send down fire to lick up the waiting sacrifice?

The Baal worshipers went first, crying out from morning till noon, pleading, begging, running around, imploring their god to send even a spark to ignite this famine-dried tinderbox into a flame for his glory.

Elijah couldn't resist. "Keep it up!" he shouted above the din. "Either he is occupied or gone aside, or is on a journey, or perhaps he is asleep and needs to be awakened" (v. 27).

Such coaching and encouragement from the other side simply heightened their frenzied passion, so they carried on till nearly dark—screaming, pounding the ground, cutting themselves to invoke the favor of their deity.

Finally their songs and chants dissolved into silence. Flies buzzed around the now rotting carcass on the altar. They had prayed up a storm—you certainly couldn't question their zeal—but they had gotten nothing in return.

Slowly Elijah approached the waterlogged altar he had made and lifted a thirty-second prayer to the one true God of heaven. In a flash, fire fell from the sky and not only consumed the dripping ox and firewood but even the rocks, the dirt, and every drop of water that had pooled underneath.

Why would God put a story like this in the Bible? One reason is to show us that long prayers, desperate pleading, and mechanical rantings are not required to request help from our Father. This One, who treasures our intimate conversations with Him and knows what we need before we ask, is not testing our faith with word counts and endurance records. Yes, there is a certain kind of shallow reward inherent in that, but (again) it's one that we give ourselves.

God's reward is reserved for those who seek His heart, not His attention.

- Do you ever catch yourself daydreaming in the midst of your prayer time?
- Do you ever pray with your mind in neutral, virtually unaware of the words you're thinking or speaking?
- Do you ever mouth the words of a hymn but think nothing of what you're singing?
- When you close a prayer "in Jesus' name," are you merely repeating a phrase, or are you truly focusing on the One who has made a way for you to approach the throne?

One evening, when our oldest daughter, Kristina, was just a small child, I asked her to pray the blessing before dinner. Like most parents we had taught her several of the childhood prayers to be prayed at meals and at bedtime. But this particular night she got her memorized prayers mixed up, and instead of "God is great, God is good," she bowed her head and began to pray, "Now I lay me down to sleep." Sheepishly, she cracked one eyelid open to see if anyone else was paying attention. When she noticed that I had looked up and was observing her with a curious stare, she grinned and said, "Oops!"

All words and no heart. Gets us nowhere every time.

Prayer is a precious privilege that allows us to have direct dialogue with the Father. We can never approach it with casual indifference or blank-check repetition and expect to get the reward He graciously offers.

The Lord's Prayer

Perhaps there is no prayer, however, that has been more widely abused and mindlessly repeated than the Lord's Prayer itself. You hear it prayed at open assemblies where Christians and non-Christians alike are instructed to say or repeat it. You hear it mumbled in a church service, usually with little understanding of what we're actually promising or asking of God. Even TV and movie characters have been known to resort to it when things look bleak and personal charm has failed to solve their problems.

- Often it's prayed only in public (for effect).
- Often it's prayed without thinking (vain repetition).
- And more often, I suspect, it's not prayed at all (prayerlessness).

It is susceptible to all three mistakes of mishandled prayer.

In this book I want you to see the Lord's Prayer, not as a memorized mantra, but as a *pattern* you can use at all times, in all situations, and all day long to express prayers to God that connect and communicate.

Notice the obvious progression of the prayer—from praise, to promises, to petitions, to parting reminders. See how easily it breaks into even series of three, making it easy to use and remember.

The Three-Part Address

Our	Stresses community
Father	Stresses relationship
Who is in heaven	Stresses authority

The Three-Part Commitment

Hallowed be Your name Commitment to holiness
Your kingdom come Commitment to participation
Your will be done Commitment to obedience

The Three-Part Petition

Daily bread Trust for physical provision
Forgiveness of debts Trust for cleansing from sin
Deliverance from evil Trust for power
over temptation

The Three-Part Benediction

Yours is the kingdom Focuses on His rule
The power Focuses on His sufficiency
The glory Focuses on His presence

When we use this pattern, prayer becomes what Jesus intended it to be: a conscious, volitional opening of our lives to God as we invite Him to accomplish His purpose in and through us. It enables us to seek His resources unselfishly as we commit ourselves to the advancement of His kingdom. In this way the effectiveness of our prayer life does not depend on the amount of our faith. Such a misunderstanding subtly teaches that our works are a necessary, added ingredient to God's grace. Instead, the effectiveness of our prayer depends on God, who gives us faith in order to lead us to total dependence on Him. This faith helps us continually bear in mind both the promise and warning of Jesus:

"I am the vine, you are the branches; he who abides in Me and I in him, he bears much fruit, for apart from Me you can do nothing" (John 15:5).

The Lord's Prayer "works." It connects.
It will literally change your life.

READY TO GO?

One of my church members used to take me on short trips in his private plane. He was an accomplished, expert pilot. Yet every time before taxiing down the runway, he would always go through the same preflight checklist: Do a thorough walk around the plane to look for damage, drain the water from the fuel tank, turn the wheel to ensure good wing movement, check the rudder pedals, set the radios.

Once as we were preparing for takeoff, I remember asking him if—as flawless and professional as he was at flying—he always had to take the time to check off these most basic, nearly automatic requirements. I'll never forget his reply: "You'd better hope that I do." Even with all his experience, the only safe and practical way to begin flying an airplane was always—without fail—to work through his checklist.

Jesus has given us our checklist. And no matter how many hours we've racked up behind the prayer wheel, we never outgrow our need to follow His commands.

So come take a seat with me. We're preparing to fly.

— 2 —

GOD AND THE
FAMILY TREE

THREE REALITIES FROM THE
PRAYER OF JESUS

I'm the kind of person who likes to think out loud. Whenever I have an important decision to make, a sermon to preach, or a difficult discussion to conduct with someone, I usually prepare by talking myself through it—while I'm driving home in the car, sitting at my desk, or pacing in the living room. *How should I phrase this or that? What do I really want to say? Which things need to be stated right up front—right at the beginning?*

You've probably done that. Let's say you have an uncomfortable phone call to make—maybe to ask about a job you interviewed for two weeks ago but haven't heard a word from since. Perhaps a client is nearly six months late paying you, a fellow church member misunderstood something you said, or you've just learned that a dear friend who lives in another state has been diagnosed with cancer.

Before you make that call, because it's so important, you obviously will spend some time thinking about what you're going to say. And in particular you'll think about how you want to *begin* the conversation. Perhaps you've even picked up the phone a time or two, dialed half the number, then hung back up because . . . you just weren't ready yet.

The way you address someone matters. First things first. *Our Father in heaven . . .*

WHAT A PRIVILEGE IT IS TO BE HERE

Before we separate the first two words of the Lord's Prayer and look at each of them individually, let's first take a look at both of them together and experience the wonder of "Our Father."

Prayer is the privilege of communication between a child and the Father. It's not a human right. Not a non-negotiable demand. It's a privilege—a privilege made possible only by the redemptive work of Jesus Christ.

> We have confidence to enter the holy place
> by the blood of Jesus, by a new and living
> way which He inaugurated for us through
> the veil, that is, His flesh. (Heb. 10:19–20)

We should never go into the presence of God without remembering that we enter by virtue of His death on the cross, His Resurrection from the grave, and His ascension into heaven.

That's why we pray "in Jesus' name." Those words *mean* something. They are not the equivalent of a stamp on a letter that guarantees delivery just because we happen to put it there. Our postage was paid at a demanding price before there was ever a "Dear God" at the top. We may not say the words *"in Jesus' name"* till the end of our prayer, but praying in His name should be the attitude of our heart from the beginning.

Yet there's even more to it than that. Jesus is not merely the doorkeeper. He is not an usher who points down the hallway and tells us it's OK to go in and see the Father—though that would be unbelievable enough. The Bible says that He actually goes in with us, praying for us:

> He is able also to save forever those who draw near to God through Him, since He always lives to make intercession for them. (Heb. 7:25)

The Holy Spirit also—the third member of the Trinity—joins us as we enter the presence of the Father.

> In the same way the Spirit also helps our weakness; for we do not know how to pray as we should, but the Spirit Himself intercedes for us with groanings too deep for words. (Rom. 8:26)

You see, prayer is not something we naturally know how to do. That's why the disciples had to ask Jesus to teach them to pray. That's why all of us who have struggled with prayer continue to come back to Him, needing help, needing direction.

That's also why He has given us the example of the Lord's Prayer. That's why He has entered the holy place with the sacrifice of His perfect obedience and continues to stand at the right hand of the Father praying on our behalf. That's why the Holy Spirit Himself also intercedes for us, conforming our prayers to the flawless will of God.

Every time you pray "Our Father," you are praying a relational prayer that is absolutely assured of placing you in the holy, awesome, glorious presence of God. But you are also reminding yourself that this privilege of prayer is not a matter to be taken lightly. It cost Christ everything, and it has given us more than we could ever deserve.

THE COMMUNITY CONTEXT

Now, back to the first word—"*our.*" Have you ever noticed that all of the first person pronouns in the Lord's Prayer are plural?

- *Our* Father
- *Our* daily bread
- *Our* debts and *our* debtors
- Lead *us* not into temptation
- Deliver *us* from evil

Isn't that something? I don't know what other conclusion to draw from that except this: According to Jesus, *prayer should always remind us that we are part of a larger community of believers.* Even though we do most of our praying alone, we should continually recognize that we live and function in a much bigger box than our prayer closets.

We may have a hard time thinking in those terms today, considering how isolated and individualistic our modern culture has become. But research has shown that even being allowed to recite the Lord's Prayer at all in the early church was a privilege reserved only for those who were fully recognized members. At their first Communion following baptism, new believers were allowed for the first time to join in praying what was then known as the "disciple's prayer." And only then were they instructed to pray it daily—a mark that identified them as a part of the broader Christian community.[1] That generation understood the concept of community.

We're All in This Together

What does this idea of "community" mean today?

It means we should be praying for our Christian friends. Each of us knows certain individuals at church, in our Sunday school class, in our family or neighborhood who are experiencing difficult situations in life. Marriage problems, health concerns, financial worries, job unrest. And we, as a part of the fellowship of Christian believers, should constantly pray for one another. This serves a twin objective: First, it enables us to care for other people, uniting with them in turning to God and God alone for help and healing, encouraging both them and us to maintain a humble perspective that lets us submit, not just our dreams, but even our sufferings into His divine plans. And second, it helps us take our minds off ourselves for a change.

In fact, among the most noticeable changes you'll see in your prayer life as you begin using the Lord's Prayer as a pattern is this: You'll find yourself praying about others' needs *more* and your own needs *less*—and yet finding your personal needs met more fully than ever before. It's simply part of what happens when you begin thinking the way God thinks and seeking His kingdom above your own.

Even our personal needs become opportunities to intercede. As you pray in the context of community, even the personal requests and concerns you share with the Father can make you mindful of others who are enduring the same situations, "knowing that the same experiences of suffering are being accomplished by your brethren who are in the world" (1 Pet. 5:9). You're not the only one facing your present batch of troubles, temptations, and trials. And even though you may not know anyone by name who fits that current description, you can be sure that God knows someone . . . somewhere . . . who needs to know He cares. Consciously pray for them even as you pray for yourself.

Likewise, God's revealed truth to you should not become an end in itself. Many times God answers our prayers with a Bible verse, a passing thought, a moving message from a sermon, or a song. And often we tend to receive that word for ourselves without thinking how it might relate to others. God's truths, however, are usually more of an investment than a handout—timeless wisdom that is able not only to comfort or correct *us* but also to be communicated through us to others. When you rise up from prayer with a specific peace and empowerment from the Lord, don't just keep it to yourself. Ask God to show you someone else who needs a similar encouragement, and be watching for Him to show you where to share it to keep His investment growing.

We should remember those who are being persecuted for their faith. For most of us, Christian faith costs little in terms of safety, freedom, and employment. But for millions today—literally millions around the globe—being a Christian comes at a staggeringly high price. According to current estimates from the U.S. State Department, Christians are today suffering countless discriminations and atrocities in more than sixty countries—more than any other religious group in the world. These are our brothers and sisters in Christ, forced for no other reason than their faith to endure torture, imprisonment, harassment, and even death. By praying for them and their families to be spared such horrors and by asking God to preserve their bold witness for Christ without fear, we participate in their sufferings and experience the reward of walking in God's power ourselves. We also ask God to help them see their persecutions as blessings in disguise, "for in the same way they persecuted the prophets who were before you" (Matt. 5:12).

We should pray for those in all areas of life and ministry. Professional ministers and missionaries are not the only people serving Christ with their life's work, though these people need and depend on God as He works through our prayers. But we should also stay in prayer for those who are making an impact for God's kingdom in places outside the four walls of the church—in the state-house and the schoolroom, on the court bench and at the car plant, in the home place and at the office park. All of these are viable mission fields where God is using real people to make a real difference every day, and your prayers can play a role in making them want to get up in the morning and meet the day head-on.

When our prayers rarely escape the tight confines of our own homes, bills, and daily bread, then our prayers are too small. Why? Because we live, pray, and worship in the midst of an enormous band of believers—the ones we know by name and the millions more who share our Lord even if not our street address.

We pray for them because they need us. They pray for us because we need them. We grow larger each day by the company we keep in our prayer closets.

THE FAMILY CONNECTION

"Father."

From our standpoint in history, from a culture that has replaced formality with chat rooms and casual day, we're not surprised to hear Jesus begin His prayer addressing the God of heaven by the name "Father." But to the Jews of Jesus' day, this intimate, personal way of approaching God was unheard of.

In the Old Testament, God is seldom spoken of as Father. Nonetheless, several references are instructive:

- The prophet Isaiah declares: "You, O LORD, are our Father, our Redeemer from of old is your name" (Isa. 63:16, NIV).
- Jeremiah speaks of God's disappointment that His people would call Him "My Father" and still practice wickedness (Jer. 3:19–20).
- A similar yet more pointed reference to God as Father is found in Malachi 1:6, when God says: "A son honors his father, and a servant his master. Then if I am a father, where is My honor? And if I am a master, where is My respect?"

There was more reverent fear and distance in the mind of the first-century Jew when they thought of God. They would not have dared to address Him with such an air of familiarity as "Father."

Yet Jesus prayed like this regularly. In fact, every one of His prayers that are recorded in the Bible (except one)[2] begins with Him saying, "Father . . ."

We see this relationship most clearly, perhaps, in Jesus' agonizing prayer from the garden of Gethsemane, the night of His capture before the day of His death. His closest friends, unable to sense the gravity of the moment, had fallen sound asleep nearby when the Bible tells us:

> He went a little beyond them, and fell to the ground, and began to pray that if it were possible, the hour might pass Him by. And He was saying, "Abba! Father! All things are

THE PRAYER OF JESUS

> possible for Thee; remove this cup from Me;
> yet not what I will, but what Thou will."
> (Mark 14:35–36)

"Abba! Father!" You probably know that many scholars believe the Aramaic word *Abba* equates to the affectionate name we know today as Daddy. *Understand this as the radical statement it was—and is!*

Jesus spoke to His Father the way we would speak to our dads—in the tender, trusting, respectful manner you know is good, even if it doesn't mirror your own personal experience with your earthly father. He talked to Him simply, openly, honestly, securely, without any reservation or hesitation.

And by teaching His disciples to pray in this way, Jesus was authorizing them to share His sonship, to relate to the sovereign God of the universe with the intimacy of a child climbing up in his daddy's lap, throwing his arms around his neck, and telling him, "I love You."

This is not irreverence; it is relationship. And to the first-century mind, it was absolutely revolutionary.

The apostle Paul was simply astounded by it. He wrote to the church in Rome:

> For you have not received a spirit of slavery
> leading to fear again, but you have received a
> spirit of adoption as sons by which we cry
> out, "Abba! Father!" (Rom. 8:15)

That prayer of Jesus had revolutionized Paul's praying. The same God who held sway over the course of history had given him permission to call Him "Daddy."

Has any so-called god ever shown such love?

DADDY'S GIRLS

My girls are grown now. Two are off and married; one is away at college. But even now, when I think about them or hear one of their voices on the phone, I get a lump in my throat. I love them so much.

I cannot imagine a time when I would be too busy to help them or would brush them off if they needed something from me. When one of my girls calls and asks for something that I know is good and important to them, I do everything in my power to ensure they get it. I rejoice in their accomplishments, support them in their dreams and endeavors, and take a hundred times more pleasure in their successes than in any of my own.

I keep their pictures in my wallet. I know their mailing addresses and phone numbers in my head. If you were to visit my office today, you would see a crayon-etched diploma inscribed to the "World's Best Dad" hanging right along with the official university diplomas and other awards I have received.

When my girls hurt, I feel their pain.

When they cry, I weep right along with them.

When they struggle, I lie awake at night thinking about them.

Is there any doubt our Father will do any less? Doesn't this knowledge alone make you want to come into His presence and stay there throughout the day?

Daddy's Discipline

But a Father's love is not always a broad smile and an open hand. Sometimes—if His love is to be true love—it must be a knowing, penetrating look. A stern tone of voice. The disciplining finger of authority.

Yes, we should begin our prayers wrapped in the warm embrace of a Father who cares for us more deeply than anyone in this world, but we should also use the first moments of our prayer time to hear His words of warning.

We are sinners. We make mountains of mistakes. Through our words, attitudes, and motives, we many times—even if unintentionally—bring dishonor on the very Christ we claim to worship. If our Father were unwilling to bring these matters to mind, we would rarely find a reason to correct them. And if He allowed us to continue on our wayward path—for fear that He might offend us—we would find ourselves drifting further and further away from the blessed life He offers.

> God deals with you as with sons; for what son is there whom his father does not discipline? But if you are without discipline, of which all have become partakers, then you are illegitimate children and not sons. Furthermore, we had earthly fathers to discipline us, and we respected them; shall we not much rather be subject to the Father of spirits, and live? For they disciplined us for a short time as seemed best to them, but He

disciplines us for our good, so that we may share His holiness. (Heb. 12:7–10)

Being a child of God comes with not only its privileges but also its responsibilities—a sort of family accountability. To address Him as Father not only reminds us that we are welcome at His side but that we are also willing to receive His correction as one of the gifts fathers give to their kids.

Already at this early point in the prayer, we find the need to confess our faults, open our hearts, and invite the revealing searchlight of His wisdom to show us where we are straying. It is here that we repent of our sins, not wanting to squander another moment of our lives resisting the touch of His hand upon our face or hoping He didn't see what we did last night when no one was looking.

He is "our Father" and we are His children.

When was the last time you called just to say, "I love you"?

The Sovereign Provision

The final phrase of the three-part address—"Our Father *who is in heaven*"—focuses our attention on God's ability to know and care for every detail of our lives. The issue is not so much about His location as it is about His authority, not so much about where He lives as it is about what He can do.

"Our God is in the heavens; He does whatever He pleases" (Ps. 115:3). So a fair question to ask at this point is: If God knows everything, and if God can do anything, and if—as the Scripture says—"your Father knows what you need before you ask Him" (Matt. 6:8), then what's the point in praying at all?

Ask Away

First, God commands us to ask. Jesus told two parables that illustrate this point. One was about an unexpected guest who dropped in on a man and his family one night, catching them without enough food in the house to set before him. His host, though he knew the hour was late, crept out at midnight to the home of a friend, knocked on the door, and asked him for three loaves of bread. Roused from sleep, the neighbor at first showed reluctance to get out of bed, but—Jesus finishes the story—"even though he will not get up and give him anything because he is his friend, yet because of his persistence he will get up and give him as much as he needs" (Luke 11:8).

The second parable tells the story of a widow who repeatedly appealed to a local judge for legal protection against someone who was threatening her. For a good while the judge who did not fear God and did not respect man continued to put her off and dismiss her claim. But at last he relented. "Otherwise by continually coming she will wear me out" (Luke 18:5).

It's clear, then, that Jesus has instructed us not only to ask but to persist in asking.

> "Ask, and it will be given to you; seek, and you will find; knock, and it will be opened to

you. For everyone who asks receives, and he who seeks finds; and to him who knocks it will be opened." (Matt. 7:7–8)

The characters in Jesus' stories were in need, but they knew exactly where to go for help. Were it not for the humble task of asking, the man would have had to send his tired guest to bed hungry. Were it not for the courage of daily perseverance, the widow might have lost all her possessions to a ruthless opponent. They both exercised their dependence on one who had the power and authority to help them, and they both received as much as they needed from his hand.

Since we know that our Father gives good gifts to His children, we should continue to pray—even when we don't get an answer the first day—so that we are not tempted to try to get our needs met somewhere else.

Maintain Your Focus

The second reason for praying to God—who already knows what you need before you ask Him—is to focus, not on our *needs,* but on our *provider.* If you look carefully at the Lord's Prayer, you will notice that the overwhelming focus is always on the Father and His kingdom, not on me and mine. In fact, all of the prayers of Jesus carry this unselfish tone and emphasis. As I began to evaluate my own prayer life under this lens, which totally reverses the way we commonly think and act, I made a painful discovery: Much of my praying had become *me-centered.*

Prayer must be *God-centered* and *kingdom-focused*. In order to approach God properly, we must be constantly looking at Him and not at our needs.

If you're a golfer, you know how it feels to walk up to a short par-3 that would ordinarily be easy to drive—except this time, a large water hazard lies between you and the green. So often in that situation you'll catch yourself digging into your bag for an old, cut-up ball, not wanting to take a chance on losing a good one under a lily pad.

Really, there's no difference in form or follow-through that distinguishes this 150-yard iron shot from another. Head down, shoulders square, left elbow straight. The only difference that could possibly enter the equation is this: your focus. Are you swinging to hit the green or to avoid the water?

Our prayers can become like that. We can spend so much time worrying about our own needs and wants and wishes that we rarely look beyond them—to the One who has promised to provide all our needs "according to His riches in glory in Christ Jesus" (Phil. 4:19).

> "If you then, being evil, know how to give good gifts to your children, how much more will your Father who is in heaven give what is good to those who ask Him!" (Matt. 7:11)

Unlike us human fathers, whose desire to give good gifts to our children is tempered by a limited amount of ability and resources, the Scripture teaches that our Father owns "the cattle on a thousand hills" (Ps. 50:10).

There is no shortage of supply that stops the love of God from showering us with everything we need in order to live as He wants us to.

This doesn't mean that we are not to ask and receive; it just means we are to seek *Him* instead of His *blessings.* Then watch the miracle that happens:

> "Your heavenly Father knows that you need all these things. But seek first His kingdom and His righteousness, and all these things will be added to you." (Matt. 6:32b–33)

When we focus on *our* kingdom—being as self-centered and shortsighted as we are—we still find ourselves distressed, incomplete, and unsatisfied. But when we focus on *God's* kingdom, He has promised to take care of our kingdom. That sounds like a pretty good deal to me.

Crossing the Line

I have found that my job in prayer is not to *inform* God; it is to *enjoy* God. And as I have approached the Father in this way, with all my attention on Him and His kingdom, I have discovered . . .

- my focus is on Him, not me.
- my heart beats for others, not just myself.
- I feel at home in His presence; I don't avoid Him out of fear or boredom.

I have found that I love to pray and that I live to pray.

In Corrie Ten Boom's gripping autobiography, *The Hiding Place,* which tells of her family's efforts to shelter Jews from the Nazi forces in Holland during World

War II, she describes in disturbing detail the conditions of the German concentration camps where she and her sister Betsie were interred for their role in the Resistance. Upon their arrival at Ravensbruck they discovered that they had landed in hell. It was a vicious labor camp where whatever shred of human dignity wasn't stripped down to the shoes at the entry gate ended up in a pile of charred bones in the gas chamber.

She walks us into the rancid dormitory, where the smell of raw sewage and soiled bedding was so overpowering it took her breath. Narrow tiers of rotting bunk platforms were so hopelessly overcrowded, the prisoners had to sleep with others' feet in their faces and knees in their backs.

And the fleas. Everywhere—biting, infested fleas.

She wailed to her sister, "What are we going to do? This is more than I can bear! How can we live in such a place?"

Betsie's reply came in short, wondering tones: "Show us. Show us how."

Corrie writes, "She said it so matter of factly that it took me a second to realize she was praying. More and more the distinction between prayer and the rest of life seemed to be vanishing for Betsie."[3]

And so it does for those of us who approach our Father in heaven through His Son, on His terms, in His love. The fleas do not become the issue—perhaps, like for Betsie, the fleas become a reason for renewed faith—but the issue becomes our faithful Father.

"Our Father in heaven."

3

ANYTIME, ANYWHERE

THREE RESPONSIBILITIES FROM THE PRAYER OF JESUS

For years I prayed the Lord's Prayer in a mechanical fashion, paying little attention to what I was actually saying.

- I would pray, "Hallowed be Your name," as if I were giving God my permission for His name to be declared holy.
- I would pray, "Your kingdom come," as if I were giving God my OK for Him to perform His sovereign work.
- I would pray, "Your will be done," as if His will were some generic concept totally disconnected from my own life.

But suddenly it dawned on me how naïve and foolish my praying had been.

- God's name is holy because God *by nature* is holy.
- God's kingdom will come whether *I* advance it or not.
- God can accomplish His will *with* me or *without* me.

So then, what do these clauses from Jesus' prayer really mean?

THE COMMITMENT CLAUSE

I believe these three statements are best understood as personal *commitments* on our part to hallow God's name in our lives, to participate in the spread of His kingdom, and to become actively involved in doing His will.

And the phrase "on earth as it is in heaven" modifies all three. This carries the meaning of *total commitment*. It's similar to Paul's appeal for us to present ourselves as "a living and holy sacrifice" to God (Rom. 12:1). This is normative Christian living and proper Christian praying.

For example, as we pray about God's will, we should ask ourselves, "How is God's will accomplished in heaven?" The answer is simple: completely, immediately, and perfectly. So as He begins to reveal His will in our lives, it's pretty clear how we should respond: completely, immediately, and perfectly.

Now, when we understand these statements not as requests but as responsibilities, several important things begin to happen:

First, we ask God to train us to look at the world from His point of view. It would be so pleasant to think that this world is filled with good, decent people who—with a little goal-setting practice and polishing up—could enjoy the multiplied blessings of the Christian life. But God teaches us through His Word that this is sadly not the case. Even some of the nice people who recycle their newspapers and keep their yard trimmed and volunteer to pick up litter by the roadside are held hostage by the power of evil. Even those of us who have been freed from Satan's grip by the grace of God must constantly fight the undertow of his lies and temptations. And everywhere—from the evening news to the grocery store aisle—we see the hideous hold that the devil has on our culture, our common sense, and even our kids. Therefore, our desire for God to reveal His name on earth has a reason much bigger than our devotional time and our church services. It has names and faces and family members and coworkers—people who desperately need to see God's name revealed as the answer for all their questions.

Second, despite the evil we witness around us, we know for a fact that God's promises are true and His victory is certain. How easy it would be the older we get to throw our hands up and surrender the battle. When the Supreme Court declares public witness to God's commandments unconstitutional, when an elderly woman is killed for the few dollars in her purse, when children are forced by necessity to practice lockdown drills as part of their school day, we wonder how much worse it could possibly get. But we will not forget this: God has promised to administer justice and to preserve His people who endure to the end. His kingdom is here and His kingdom is coming. And no devil in hell can do anything to stop it.

Third, we acknowledge God's call on our lives to be His instruments. He could expand His kingdom and bring all things into submission to His will without using any of us, but God's delight and plan is to empower and enable us to be messengers of hope in our decaying world. The material things we see around us on this earth will not survive eternity, but the souls of those within range of our lunchroom conversations, our morning walks, and our compassionate touch bear the possibility of a glorious forever. When we commit our lives into God's service, He compensates us in eternal dividends. It's astounding what He chooses to do through us.

Finally, we avoid asking for anything that would dishonor God's name, delay His kingdom, or thwart His will. In other words, we begin operating daily from a Christian worldview, letting God take care of our kingdoms while we concentrate our full attention on His. Again, it's "praying without ceasing," letting His presence permeate our thoughts and actions all day long—anytime, anywhere.

HALLOWED BE YOUR NAME

Jesus turns our attention first to the Father's name—His *hallowed* name. The word literally means "to make holy" or "to treat as holy." In heaven this very hour, the angels are singing to the Father in joyous wonder: "Holy, holy,

holy," extolling this One who is worthy of all praise and adoration.

But not only is the *Father* holy; His *name* is holy.

One of the reasons I wrote the book *The Names of God* was to capture some of the awe and wonder expressed through the different titles ascribed to Him in Scripture. There are dozens of vivid, descriptive names that apply to every situation you face in life.

For example, when you or someone you love is ill, you can pray to Him knowing that He is Jehovah-Rophe: "The Lord heals." When you find yourself in the grip of temptation, you can sense His strength, victory, and protection by giving thanks to Him for being Jehovah-Nissi: "The Lord Our Banner." He is . . .

- Jehovah-Shammah: "The Lord Is There."
- Jehovah-M'Kaddesh: "The Lord Who Sanctifies."
- El-Elyon: "The Lord Most High."

A more complete list is in the appendix of this book, which you will find helpful as you focus on His name throughout the day.

But there's more than praise and worship involved in hallowing the name of God.

The Family Name

The day I left home for college to play football at Wake Forest University, I remember my dad walking me to the car to give me my "going off to college" lecture. You know the one.

My mom had decided to play it safe by staying behind on the porch. I could see her crying by the back door. And as I turned to hear what Dad had to say, I braced myself for what I thought could be a pretty long speech.

But instead his words were surprisingly brief. He said, "Son, I have only one piece of advice to give you. I want to remind you that you bear my name. Your great-grand-father was a church planter and preacher; your grandfather was a godly man, and I think you know I've tried to live faithfully before God. *The name Hemphill stands for something.* So don't take my name anywhere I wouldn't take it, and don't involve my name in anything I wouldn't do." And with that the going-away speech was over.

But not really. For although I didn't grasp at the time how important his advice would become, that reminder helped me many times through the years to make difficult but appropriate decisions when there was no one around to tell me what to do or how to behave.

You see, our family reputation was at stake. Our name would be judged by the things I did and the places I went. I didn't have to worry so much about the specifics of splitting hairs or skirting the gray areas. I just had to see Dad's face in my mind, and I always knew without a doubt what I was supposed to do.

In the same way, you and I bear the name of our heavenly Father. Therefore, everywhere we go and everything we do casts a reflection on Him.

Everywhere. Everything.

So in the morning when I get up and at frequent times throughout the day, I pray, "Father, hallowed be your name"—in *my* life, in your *people's* lives.

What does that do? How does that prayer connect?

- It's the kind of prayer I find rewarded when the cleaners have ruined one of my shirts and I'm tempted to take my anger out on the girl at the cash register. *Hallowed be Your name.* I don't want the stain of my bad witness to come off on Christ.

- It's the kind of prayer I find rewarded when the plane is delayed and I doubt there's any way I can make my connecting flight. *Hallowed be Your name.* I don't want to blow my chance right out of the gate to share Christ with the man sitting in the seat next to me.

- It's the kind of prayer I find rewarded when I'm away from home and anonymous in an airport magazine shop. *Hallowed be Your name.* I don't want my eyes to lead me astray or give me away.

Unfortunately, a lot of Christians have had a negative impact on the gospel, not by deliberately blaspheming God's name but by not being careful to live up to their calling at the gym or the office or the Little League diamond. Hallowing God's name is a commitment that has anytime/anywhere implications.

What's in a Name?

I know how important this matter of reputation was to *my* father. But it is of even greater importance to our *heavenly* Father.

In Ezekiel, chapter 36, the prophet is rebuking Israel for their unrighteous behavior that has sullied the name of God and forced Him to punish them severely by banishing them into exile. But almost in the same breath (as he speaks the words of God) Ezekiel declares:

> "I will vindicate the holiness of My great name which has been profaned among the nations, which you have profaned in their midst. Then the nations will know that I am the LORD . . . when I prove Myself holy among you in their sight." (Ezek. 36:23)

The fact that Israel had profaned God's name was an established fact in His eyes. And the last thing they deserved was to be delivered from the captivity they had brought on themselves. Nevertheless, God promised to gather His people from the shackles of slavery and restore them to their homeland. Why? Because He was unwilling for the other nations to persist in mocking *His name,* to consider His arm too weak to save or His power no match for the armies of men. His name was at stake.

In Jesus' remarkable high-priestly prayer found in John 17, He summarizes the most important aims of His earthly ministry:

> "I have manifested Your name to the men whom You gave Me out of the world; . . . I have made Your name known to them, and will make it known, so that the love with which You loved Me may be in them, and I in them." (John 17:6, 26)

Of all the things Christ had accomplished, among the most crucial was that He had put a face on the name of God. And so do we—every time we keep our cool, maintain our integrity, and honor our commitment to hallow His name.

Your Kingdom Come

My wife and I were in China recently with several other seminary presidents. Our stated task was to visit a number of seminaries and Bible colleges in China to see if there was any way we could assist them in theological training. Because we were escorted from appointment to appointment, we had little opportunity to interact with the Chinese people. But even if we had, the language presented a formidable barrier.

I assumed that the entire kingdom perspective of our visit would be lived out in the years ahead as we assisted men and women with their studies. But the trip we took from Nanjing to Shanghai was by train, and we shared the ride with two young Chinese adults who were seated across the table from us. Paula soon discovered that the young woman spoke English very well. In fact, she was a communications major who enjoyed every opportunity to practice her English.

So with the language barrier removed, we talked. We laughed. We shared. We asked questions. And near the end of our conversation, as we were exchanging E-mail addresses and promising to keep in touch, I asked if I could give her a little booklet that explained our philosophy of life. *Yes! She'd be glad to receive it.* And she enthusiastically took the *GotLife* tract[1] I had recently written, which communicates the truths about the abundant Christian life. And once again Paula and I discovered that the kingdom comes in unexpected ways and at unusual times—when we've made a commitment to be looking for it.

Coming Attractions

Simply stated, the kingdom of God is "His rule." Just as the king of a country has the total right and authority to govern his subjects, the coming of our Father's kingdom will bring about the full reign of God when it is ultimately consummated at the end of time. So when we pray, "Your kingdom come," we are in part looking for— yes, *longing for* that final establishment of God's rule over all His creation.

In a real sense the kingdom is already a present reality. John the Baptist warned the citizens of his day to "repent, for the kingdom of heaven is at hand" (Matt. 3:2). And with the commencement of Jesus' ministry on earth, the kingdom indeed began to grow and expand.

You can see both of these perspectives—both the present and the future—in Christ's parable of the wheat and the tares (Matt. 13:24–30, 36–43). It's the story of a man who planted his crops in the field, but during the night an enemy sneaked onto his land and randomly scattered some *other* kinds of seed across the hungry soil. As the weeks passed, the wheat began to grow—just as the farmer hoped it would—but signs of another harvest were also tangled throughout his field:

the unwelcome invasion of weeds planted by a jealous neighbor.

"How did this happen? And what should we do about it?" the laborers asked, angry at the extra work involved in weeding a plant bed so knotted with wild grass. The landowner wisely instructed them to "allow both to grow together until the harvest," not wanting to harm the good crops on account of the bad. Not until the final harvest would he pull up the weeds and burn them in their own pile, leaving the ripe, mature wheat crop to be gathered and stored.

Jesus went on to explain that the good seeds represent the "sons of the kingdom." That means us—present-day followers of Christ already growing in the world, as well as all who have lived before and all who will come to Christ in the days ahead. But the kingdom concept is also seen in the future harvest time, when—with all the weeds removed—"the righteous will shine forth as the sun in the kingdom of their Father."

While God's kingdom is a coming event, it is also a present reality.

So when we pray, "Your kingdom come," we are at one moment recognizing the fact that God's ultimate rule is simply a matter of time, and we are also committing ourselves to participate in seeing it unfold before our eyes. And that is what's really exciting!

Heaven in the Real World

This aspect of the Lord's Prayer continues to amaze me, not only because I missed the point for so long, but also because I now realize that it places me right on the cutting edge of kingdom living all day, every day.

Again, just as the line between prayer and life begins to vanish through the "praying without ceasing" mentality of the Lord's Prayer, this kingdom focus dissolves the hard line between sacred and secular. If you take a good look at Jesus' life, you see that *all* of it was sacred. Every event and occurrence in His life, no matter how ordinary or offhand, had a kingdom priority to it.

His *disciples* didn't always understand this. They would shoo the children away to keep Him on schedule, and hustle the crowds along so they could get some rest. But Jesus saw everything through the lens of the Father's kingdom. Even with this sense of divine urgency, He never appeared rattled, stressed out, or in a hurry. He simply watched to see where the kingdom was working, and He moved toward it with eyes and arms wide open. And so can we.

Everywhere we go has kingdom implications. And if our heart's desire is constantly trained to see His kingdom come, we'll be ready to share the hope of the gospel with anyone we meet, anywhere we are.

- When you stop for gas on the way home, *Your kingdom come.* You're watching, looking, expecting an opportunity to hear something, to say something.
- When you take your family out to dinner, *Your kingdom come.* The waiter, the busboy, the woman who seats you, the people waiting with you for a table. Are they open to a conversation? Has the

Spirit placed the two of you here on this night, at this hour, in this particular circumstance?

- When you're running on the treadmill, *Your kingdom come.* When you finally stop long enough to cool down and catch your breath, will someone be waiting? Someone worrying? Someone wanting to know that God is real and that He really cares?

Now am I suggesting that He wants to take all the fun out of your life, that never again can you simply go for a walk, or vacation at the beach, or kick back and relax without constantly feeling on call? Of course God understands your need for fun and rest. Remember the verse we looked at earlier, the one you probably know by heart:

> "Your heavenly Father knows that you need all these things. But seek first His kingdom and His righteousness, and all these things will be added to you." (Matt. 6:32b–33)

As you seek His kingdom, you can quit worrying about yours. If you'll focus on His thoughts and desires, *your Father* will make sure that you get enough sleep, that a skipped meal won't kill you, that you and your family will have all the time together you need. *You can't get in any better hands than His—not even your own!*

And so you are free to approach even your fun times as kingdom events:

- When you're away on vacation, let God use you to bring home a lot more than a well-read novel and a suntan. Bring home the blessing of sharing Christ with someone you never would have had the chance to meet in your everyday routine.

• When your family gets together for a holiday, let God use you to interject hope and truth into conversations about world events and bear-market reports. See if it can't be the kind of homecoming for a lost relative or in-law that will make your family gathering the best one you've ever had.

Because the kingdom is here. Because the kingdom is coming.

And you have suddenly become an active part of it.

YOUR WILL BE DONE

The third commitment is similar to the one before, except that—like the "hallowed be your name" pledge—it requires much more than your ears, your mind, and your mouth. It requires all of you, all the time.

When you pray, "Your will be done," throughout the day, you are committing yourself not only to His kingdom but also to the full accomplishment of His will in your life. And this has major implications!

Now let me warn you right up front: *This will not be convenient.* These commitments demand that your own needs and emotions take a backseat to God's desires for your life. But does anything that is truly worthwhile require any less?

If you can be brave enough to look into the future and compare what your life will be like when you: (a) let

God have control of your time and activities, or (b) waste it on your own self-interests, you will see that God's ways lead to a life of blessing, joy, and no regrets.

This prayer makes every moment of every day an *adventure* with the Father. No two days of yours will ever be alike again! To the ordinary mind, this responsibility may seem like slavery. But I can assure you that it is the most freeing experience you will ever know. And you get to enjoy it every day as you come to enjoy Him every moment.

A Change in Plans

First, however, you need to see God's will in a much bigger perspective than the way most people usually think of it. Deciding which school to attend, choosing whom to marry, or considering God's call to the mission field are certainly decisions to be made in accordance with His will. But major milestones like these are not the *only* arenas where it's necessary to discern the plans of God. That could happen at any point of your day, every day of your life.

Let's say, for example, that around 2:00 one afternoon—in the midst of a long day at work—I start thinking that as soon as I leave the office in three or four hours, I'm going to go home, change clothes, and treat myself to some time at the driving range. Ah—my day is starting to pick up *already*. The rest of the afternoon and the whole way home, I can already feel the club in my hand, hear the whip of my swing, see the ball soaring long and straight and beyond the yardage markers.

But suppose that when I get home, as I'm loosening my necktie and fumbling for a comfortable shirt, I find that my wife has also had a frustrating day. Things haven't gone well. A new problem has arisen. She needs to talk. She needs me to listen.

Whose kingdom is going to win? Whose needs are going to get met? Whose will is going to prevail over the other's? Mine? Or hers? What if God knows that what I *really* need this evening is not the pleasure of connecting with a golf ball but the responsibility of connecting with my wife?

Good questions, aren't they? And though I think we all know the right answers, we don't always quiet our growling appetites long enough to do the right thing.

So does this mean I never get to do what I want to do? Of course not. It simply means that I choose to put the full responsibility for that on God's shoulders because I trust Him to make sure I get all the recreation I need.

Therefore, the right question to ask myself at 2:00 in the afternoon is not "Wonder if I can get to the driving range by 5:30?" but "Lord, will you keep me open to your will—whatever that is for this evening?" Because anywhere *in* the will of God is better than anywhere else *outside* of it.

A Full Day of Appointments

Let me show you how much fun this can be.

Not too long ago I spoke during the weekly chapel service at LifeWay Christian Resources in Nashville. As

I was chatting with people at the door following my sermon, a young man stopped to talk with me. He said, "I'm so glad I got to see you today. In fact, for a long time I've been meaning to write and thank you for what you've meant to my life."

Seeing my delighted but perplexed expression, he went on: "We were members at First Baptist Church in Woodstock, Georgia, when you and Paula were there. I knew you only by sight because you weren't able to be in church very often with your busy travel schedule. But one Sunday after the service, you invited my wife and me to your home. I told you that I was struggling with God's will for my life and trying to figure how He might put my business experience to better use. You and your wife counseled with us and prayed for us before we left for home that day. The Lord used some of the things you said to redirect our lives. I believe I'm working here today because of the things you helped me see that Sunday afternoon."

That would make anybody feel good.

A few weeks later I was preaching in Florida. My host told me that one of the staff members at the church had asked if he might take me out to breakfast. *Sure!* During our early morning conversation the next day, the man began to share how God had used me to save his ministry. Several years before, I had been speaking at a Sunday school conference in his state, and he had been assigned to pick me up at the airport. Realizing we had a few hours before the conference began, I had suggested we stop somewhere and get a cup of coffee. For two hours that day he had poured his heart out to me about his disappointments, his disillusionments, his discouragements. At that time he was serving at a church in bitter turmoil, but in those stolen moments in a little coffee shop, God had touched his heart and changed his focus. Instead of giving up, he had dug in. God had blessed his life and ministry with a new vision for reaching out and loving people.

If I had been plotting my schedule that day, those two hours would have fallen under the category "on the way to the conference." Instead, those were two divinely appointed hours that were just as important as the official business of the day. I didn't catalog either event in my memory bank, yet God used the "Your will be done" commitment to advance His kingdom and to honor His name.

And it happens like that all the time—on the way, in the process, while we wait.

By the Way

Remember the day in Jesus' life when the ruler, Jairus, rushed up to Him, fell at His feet, and pleaded with Him to come to his sick daughter's bedside? All of us can identify with this father's sense of urgency—his daughter left behind at home, lingering at death's door. We too would have begged Jesus to *please, please come quickly!*

Jesus got up to go with him, but somewhere along the way between where He was and where He was going, a woman who had suffered with internal bleeding for twelve years summoned the strength to work her way through the crowd and quietly touch the hem of His garment. She didn't want to bother Him, would never have intentionally interrupted His visit to Jairus's house, didn't know how she would react in public to being healed of her disease, didn't want to be embarrassed by suddenly becoming the center of attention.

Perhaps that's why she chose this moment. She was probably unaware of the crisis that caused the hurried pace of the Master. Had she known the urgency of the moment, she never would have dared to divert Him from His mission.

But isn't it interesting that the Master would slow His pace at a time like this to touch a little old woman with her little old problems—when Resurrection was on the calendar?

But He did stop. He did notice. His kingdom business had been current the moment Jairus skidded hard into the dust at His feet, but it would also be current at this moment, with this woman. God's name would be declared holy at both places that day—both *at* Jairus's house and *on the road* to Jairus's house.

"Your kingdom come, Your will be done." That's all that matters.

- When you're waiting somewhat impatiently in the doctor's office, *Your will be done.* Even if you're worried about your blood work. Even if all is quiet and others might overhear. What year-old magazine is worth missing the will of God?
- When you're wondering why you're wasting time at a social function you "had to attend," *Your*

kingdom come. Your will be done. Hallowed be Your name, Father. Right over the punch bowl.

You won't have more time later. It won't get any more convenient later.

It's now. It's here.

It's not you. It's Him.

And it's the most fun you'll ever have as a Christian—watching God turn your every day into an everyday adventure.

4

I'VE GOT YOU COVERED

THREE REQUESTS FROM THE PRAYER OF JESUS

We move now to the moment where we crawl up into our Father's lap and bring before Him our daily needs. Our God who asks so much of us knows that we can do nothing without His help and provision. So we can pray to Him knowing that He is not only *aware* of our needs but also *able* to meet them—*wanting* to meet them.

He loves us so deeply that He would never give us anything that's out of line with who we are, what we're going through, and what He has called us to be. As praying children, we have already committed ourselves in the previous section of the Lord's Prayer to seek the Father's will continually. Now this same family bond gives us the freedom to ask "whatever we will" with the confidence that the Father will answer our petitions out of His heavenly wisdom and according to His understanding of our needs.

STANDING IN THE NEED OF PRAYER

Think back to the last time you tried breaking a bad habit or committing to a good one, and you'll agree with me that *saying* you'll do something and actually *doing* it are two different things. Not that it's impossible to effect a genuine change in your focus or behavior—it can certainly be done—but it takes a lot more than sheer guts and willpower to do it. Success in a noble endeavor requires the joint forces of both heart and mind. And nowhere is that more evident than in the Christian's life.

A believer who is clinging to bitterness and unforgiveness, for example, cannot consistently achieve the goals of loving others unconditionally or being less judgmental. A person wanting to be more serious about prayer and Bible study but unwilling to give up a known habit of lust or laziness will invariably find that two desires going in opposite directions cannot coexist for long without the one that's easier winning.

So when we who have entrusted our lives into the hands of God strive to make the kind of radical commitments we talked about in the last chapter, we need much more than a hearty zeal and a head of steam. We need help from God—help that goes right to the bone, to the soul, to the spirit. Our Father understands that.

Therefore, He has given us permission to ask Him to meet every possible need we will ever experience.

That's because He knows that the needs we possess in one part of our lives will have an impact on another. A constantly worried mind will put a strain on our physical health. A frequently empty stomach will cloud our ability to think clearly. A brewing, angry temper will eventually show itself in acts of rage and aggression. All of these dampen our ability to seek His kingdom.

We need help to live the Christian life—the deep-down help that only God can give—and we need it now. So Jesus instructs us to ask . . . for everything.

- For our *bodies*—the sustenance of daily bread.
- For our *souls*—the peace of a clear conscience.
- For our s*pirits*—the freedom to willfully obey.

For every dimension of our human existence.

His Name, His Claim

But I want to warn you not to confuse the bold petitions found in the Lord's Prayer with the false "name it and claim it" prosperity gospel that has pervaded the church in our day. Our requests for daily bread, forgiveness of sins, and deliverance from evil are not selfish demands; instead they are *understood requirements* for serving in His kingdom. They are not promises held over God's head to insist that He treat us to a certain level of lifestyle, but expressions of total dependence on Him for each day's provision.

We can agree that the Father loves us deeply, wants to bless us, and desires that we have everything in His storehouse that is intended for us. Furthermore, we can agree that we don't have to beg or whine like spoiled children to receive such favor; rather, it is His good pleasure to shower these blessings on us.

One of God's main purposes in supplying our human needs is to enable us to fulfill the kingdom commitments we've made. The commitments we've made enable us to focus our prayers and our lives on God, the giver, not on the size or specifics of His gifts. Remember—again:

> "Your heavenly Father knows that you need all these things. But seek first His kingdom and His righteousness, and all these things will be added to you." (Matt. 6:32b–33)

We are not self-seeking when we ask the Father to meet our physical, emotional, and spiritual needs. We are merely asking for the strength needed to fulfill our kingdom responsibilities. We are kingdom-seeking.

Jesus promises that if we as His followers will focus on His kingdom, He will personally manage the affairs of our own kingdoms.

When we attempt to manage our own kingdom affairs, we become fretful and anxious because we have no power to control all the situations that come about or to alter our circumstances. Jesus understands this: "Who of you by worrying can add a single hour to his life?" (Matt. 6:27, NIV).

So in response He gives us an offer we should be unable to refuse: *You focus on My kingdom, and I in turn will manage your kingdom.*

What could possibly be more liberating than that?

On Earth as It Is in Heaven

One day in the future—when God's kingdom has come in all its fullness—we will be free from all the conditions that require these requests.

- We will no longer need to ask for "our daily bread," because our physical needs will be met simply by being in His tangible presence.
- There will be no sin, no broken relationships that require Him to "forgive us our debts as we forgive our debtors."
- Our freedom from temptation and our deliverance from evil will be a moot point, for no desire to do wrong will even exist when God's heavenly reign is complete.

Despite the fact that we can only partially know this kind of freedom while we're here on earth, *Jesus allows us to pray that these kingdom realities will invade our daily living now!* By "praying without ceasing" and trusting Him for everything, we citizens of the kingdom can progressively experience God's presence and provision in our daily lives right now—for *His* name, for *His* honor, for *His* glory! In a world where God seems remote, where sin enslaves, where hunger and thirst are everyday realities, His children can experience the current invasion of kingdom provision.

Isn't that just like Jesus?

Already He's taught us that in His kingdom, leaders serve. Givers receive. The last are first and the first are last. Those who mourn are comforted. Those who hunger are filled. Those who suffer persecution are blessed beyond measure.

Isn't it just like Jesus to continue the paradigm shift—not only to reverse our normal way of thinking but also to bend the constraints of time and space and transport the realities of the future into our present-day experience?

That's what happens as we bring our requests to the Father. That's what happens as He meets our needs in His loving, powerful way.

That's the exciting truth of this pattern of prayer.

Our Daily Bread

In order to think and pray this way, we must first shake off the false notion that life is somehow separated into two distinct compartments—the secular and the sacred—and that the practical needs of everyday life occupy one place, while Christian faith and its responsibilities occupy another.

The early church didn't see it that way. When you read Paul's words in chapter eleven of 1 Corinthians (vv. 17–34), you get the idea that the first-century Christians combined their Lord's Supper observances with the enjoyment of a potluck dinner. That observation is not far from the truth. The "breaking of bread" was a crucial part of their lives together, for it helped sustain many of the early believers who were living hand to mouth. Their gatherings had both *physical* and *spiritual* significance.

Paul's concern in the first part of that passage was not that they were eating supper at a time set aside for spiritual things. His problem was this: The wealthy were not sharing their abundance with those in need, "for in your eating each one takes his own supper first; and one is hungry and another is drunk" (v. 21). Since their fellowship meals intertwined the material with the spiritual, their lack of regard for others' physical needs brought reproach on the name of God. Even *this* meal, you see, was "the Lord's Supper" (v. 20).

Today we have lost much of this understanding—that all things fall under the category of *sacred* in the believer's life. For Jesus' followers in every generation, there should be no distinction between the two.

Daily bread and kingdom commitments don't live on separate streets. They live right in the middle of the intersection.

Father Nature

Your Father knows that you have a life. That life includes cereal on the breakfast table, diapers on the baby, a coat on your back, and a pair of decent shoes on your feet. It includes a roof over your head and the money to keep it there, a job to work and the opportunity to excel, a car that runs and a reliable mechanic to help it stay that way.

To most people there is nothing spiritual about these things, nothing sacred about writing the check for this month's rent, eating a tuna sandwich, or fixing a leaky faucet. But for us as Christians, these routine matters provide ongoing evidence that a compassionate, loving God cares about the most ordinary matters in our lives.

Hard to believe? Jesus says to take a lesson from nature.

> "Look at the birds of the air, that they do not sow, nor reap nor gather into barns, and yet your heavenly Father feeds them. Are you not worth much more than they? . . .
>
> And why are you worried about clothing? Observe how the lilies of the field grow; they do not toil nor do they spin, yet I say to you that not even Solomon in all his glory clothed himself like one of these. But if God so clothes the grass of the field, which is alive today and tomorrow is thrown into the furnace, will He not much more clothe you? You of little faith!" (Matt. 6:26, 28–30)

We are often guilty of asking the question, "What's in it for us?" But when we ask that question while intentionally focusing our attention on the kingdom of God, here's the incredible answer we receive: *"Everything!"* God delights in taking care of everything we need, as long as we realize that the things we receive from Him are *equipment,* not decorations. His provision gives us the security of being better prepared, not the cheap thrill of making a better impression.

Worry Free

Furthermore, by taking responsibility for our personal, physical needs, God actually declares a ban on worry.

Jesus refers to *anxiety* five times in the short passage that follows closely after the Lord's Prayer (Matt. 6:25–32). And in three of those occurrences He literally uses an imperative term that amounts to a *commandment* not to worry.

This is not just a sweet, Sunday morning idea. He is serious. God has eliminated our need for worry.

Because our focus is so often on ourselves, because our prayers are so *me-* and *mine-centered,* because we don't really believe that we can count on God to watch out for us if we turn our back on our own concerns to "seek first His kingdom," even our prayer lives can become worry central. Many times, we are strangely more anxious *in* prayer than we are *out* of prayer.

It's human nature, of course. As the Bible says, "The Gentiles eagerly seek all these things," always needing a month's supply stored away in order to rest easy in their minds. But God has chosen to have a relationship with us that transforms the natural. "Your heavenly Father knows that you need all these things" (Matt. 6:32). This does not mean we shouldn't plan wisely, save money, and invest well. It does mean, however, that we cannot allow a reliance on our own income potential to replace our daily dependence on the Lord.

So we are instructed simply to ask Him for our daily bread, and as we do . . .

We are made aware that every meal we enjoy is eaten in His presence and provided by His hand. "For He has satisfied the thirsty soul, and the hungry soul He has filled with what is good" (Ps. 107:9).

We are reminded that Jesus Himself is "the bread of life; he who comes to Me will not hunger, and he who believes in Me will never thirst" (John 6:35).

We learn to trust God for each day's amount, just as Israel had to depend on God to provide manna from heaven to feed them during their wanderings in the wilderness. God warned them not to store their manna for the coming day—anything left overnight would be spoiled by morning—because He not only desired to provide for their nourishment but also to teach them that they could trust His daily provision sight unseen.

We turn our back on the allure of riches, refusing to become dependent on our own resources—not just our money and our income-earning potential but also our family connections, our professional position, our personal charm. We depend on God alone for every aspect of our daily lives, trusting Him only for the things we need.

We recognize that the personal pronoun in this prayer is plural—that we are committed to sharing with those who do not have adequate provision. We know that God will provide us enough for the next day, so we are free to share our excess with anyone who may not have enough bread for *this* day.

All of life, you see, is a sacred trust.

Do you see the difference inherent in this kind of praying? Do you ever want to settle again for a prayer life that's always asking God for more stuff—for you— always for you? Don't you hunger for a relationship with God that keeps you in the center of His will instead of just keeping you happy—one that keeps you fully fed while you're fully serving? Didn't Jesus Himself say, "Whoever wishes to save his life will lose it, but whoever loses his life for My sake and the gospel's will save it" (Mark 8:35)?

Daily bread is plenty when God is your portion.

FORGIVE US OUR DEBTS

Debt is a concept we all understand. We know the extra hours that we work, the things we forego, the nights we labor over the budget trying to get the nagging monster of debt off our backs. It worries us even when we're not thinking about it.

But when was the last time your *sin* kept you up at night? Not because you were ashamed of yourself, not because you didn't like the conflict it had created, but just because you realized that you were *in debt to God*—because you had grieved His Holy Spirit—because you had tarnished His hallowed name?

Sin is serious—*always* serious—because it drives a wedge between us and our Father. The time we spend in debt to God is time we spend away from Him. And the time we spend away from Him is time we waste forever.

Clinging to sin and seeking His kingdom cannot happen at the same time.

Debt Free

So if we are going to fulfill the three commitments we have made to God, this petition to "forgive us our debts" must be given equal weight with our request for "daily bread"—our rent, food, and clothing. Yes, God wants us to have four good walls and grocery money. But for us to be useful instruments in His hand, we desperately need the freedom of a clear conscience. If we hide our sin or attempt to deny its existence, we will not experience the incredible joy of knowing God's forgiveness and the full privileges of sonship.

> If we say that we have no sin, we are deceiving ourselves and the truth is not in us. If we confess our sins, He is faithful and righteous to forgive us our sins and to cleanse us from all unrighteousness. (1 John 1:8–9)

One evening years ago my older brother and I had a minor altercation at home that ended with a thrown basketball crashing into the mirror on our dresser. My dad quickly appeared on the scene. But by then the room was quiet except for two boys trying to look and sound as innocent as possible—and my brother holding the basketball. Leaping on this bit of leverage, I quickly blamed Philip for the whole affair and declared that I had nothing to do with it. So Dad took my brother out to punish him and left me alone to think about my involvement.

Well, you know how quiet that room felt. I struggled with my uneasy conscience for several hours, until finally I plucked up enough courage to walk into my father's bedroom and stutter out my confession. "Dad, I know you think Philip was responsible for the broken mirror, but I may have had something to do with it."

I'll never forget his response: "Son, I knew you were involved. I was just waiting for you to understand your guilt."

When we confess our sin to God, we don't reveal anything about us that He doesn't already know. We come before Him—this Father who loves us—with absolute honesty. We "say the same thing" He is already thinking, which is what the term *confession* literally means.

Confession is not a sweeping apology that makes us feel better on the outside while making no impact on our hearts. We must be specific as we pray this prayer throughout the day, personalizing the petition by allowing the Holy Spirit to bring areas of sinfulness to mind that are hindering our relationship with the Father and with others. When we are specific in confession—naming times and dates and details—God quickly overflows our sadness and brokenness with His overwhelming joy. We experience liberation from our debts and the restoration of intimacy that enables us to call God Father.

Anything less than full disclosure always brings less than full release.

A Classic Cover-Up

I had the joy of growing up in a Christian home with an earthly father who loved me without reservation. Spending time with him was one of my greatest joys, followed only, I suspect, by the warmth of our whole family sitting down together around the supper table every night sharing the good food, the day's events, the wonderful conversation.

I loved being called to dinner—except for this one particular evening.

Late one afternoon a bunch of us were playing outside when a buddy of mine whipped out several cigarettes he had taken from his dad's dresser. I knew I shouldn't do what he was asking. My parents drew the line of right and wrong way before a person could get around to cigarette-smoking. But the guys were all agreeing to try it. The pressure to conform was pretty intense. So I lit one up.

I had only taken a few guilty puffs before I heard the sound of my mother's voice calling me in for supper. And for the first time in my life, I had no desire to join my family. I knew that Dad would detect the smoke on my breath. He would know.

When I arrived at home, everyone had already gathered around the table. Bursting through the door, I covered my mouth and quickly ran to the bathroom with the faint excuse that I needed to wash my hands—which gave me away right there. What eight-year-old boy volunteers to wash his hands? Turning on the water to provide some background noise, I frantically began hunting for that funny-looking liquid my parents swished around in their mouths to freshen their breath. Unfortunately, though, I had not paid adequate attention to this adult ritual, and instead of locating the mouthwash, I guessed wrong with a bottle of my mother's lilac-scented toilet water. Believe me—if you've never gargled with watered-down perfume, you wouldn't do yourself any favors by starting today!

Instead of settling comfortably into my chair that night, I went to the dinner table smelling like a small garden of lilacs. Why? Because I didn't want to be in the presence of my father with the smell of cigarettes on my breath.

When we try to hide the sin in our lives rather than dealing with it honestly, we forfeit the joy of true forgiveness. When our conscience is defiled, we have no desire to be with our Father.

Come clean. Tell Him everything. He knows your need even before you agree with Him. Nothing that you can confess will surprise Him or exceed His desire and ability to forgive. Stay debt free through the day—moment by moment, at the slightest twinge from your conscience. Debt-free living enables you to hallow God's name, expand His kingdom, and do His will.

Share the Wealth

But there's more to this debt reduction than just experiencing God's forgiveness for ourselves. The request for God to "forgive us our debts" also includes the adjoining phrase—"as we forgive our debtors." Now, this shouldn't be misunderstood to mean that offering forgiveness to others is a prerequisite to our receiving it. Not at all. The Bible is absolutely clear that we can do *nothing* to earn God's forgiveness (see Rom. 5:6–8 or Eph. 2:8–9). Grace flows from His very nature. It was made available to us even when we were dead in our trespasses and sins.

Those who are willing to forgive others show that they have been truly forgiven themselves.

Jesus, again using the terminology of *debt* as a vivid description of sin, told the story of a king who decided to settle some of his slaves' outstanding accounts (Matt. 18:21–35). One of the men who appeared before him had an enormous IOU—more than he could ever hope to pay off in a lifetime. With the man facing the loss of his wife, his children, literally everything he had as terms of his repayment, he fell to his knees and pleaded for mercy. Moved with compassion, the king ordered the full amount of the man's debt to be waived—all of it. This man with the debt he could never repay suddenly owed absolutely nothing. Incredible!

But in His story Jesus followed this same man back home where a similar scene took place in reverse. This time the forgiven slave went out looking for a man who owed him a small amount—about a day's wages. You might think the relieved ex-debtor was eager to let a small measure of the grace he had just received spill over into another's life. But instead, "He seized him and began to choke him, saying, 'Pay back what you owe'" (v. 28). Again there was begging, pleading, and an appeal for mercy. But this time they fell on deaf ears as the forgiven slave turned the man over to the authorities and had him thrown into jail.

Soon the king got wind of it and called the man he had previously forgiven before him. "You wicked slave, I forgave you all that debt because you pleaded with me. Should you not also have had mercy on your fellow slave, in the same way that I had mercy on you?" (vv. 32–33).

The point of the parable is crystal clear. A true experience of grace makes us gracious in our relationships with others. When we remain unforgiving toward others who have wronged us, we have not taken seriously the enormity of our own sin and the cost that Christ has incurred to provide our forgiveness. When we refuse to forgive, we are the ones held captive.

Deliver Us from Evil

Our sin problem would be bad enough if we only had to deal with the messes we've already made. But each day we dig the hole a little deeper. Each day we run the risk of making things even worse. But God—again—can be trusted to meet all of our needs.

He knows that while empty pantries devoid of "daily bread" can make us resentful, and strained relationships not mended by forgiving "our debtors" can make us bitter, failing to live faithfully before Him robs us of both reward and reputation, of worship and witness, of courage and character.

We have a lot to lose by not obeying Him, and we don't have a prayer unless He helps us.

Nowhere Else to Hide

The quickest way to make this request a reality—not to lead us into temptation, but to deliver us from evil—is to realize that we can make no headway in holiness without God's constant provision. Not only are we no match for our adversary the devil, but we cannot even trust *ourselves* for help in keeping our lives clean:

> Let no one say when he is tempted, "I am being tempted by God"; for God cannot be tempted by evil, and He Himself does not tempt anyone. But each one is tempted when he is carried away and enticed by his own lust. (James 1:13–14)

As long as we are here on earth, we will have to contend with our enemy, with our environment, and—yes—even with ourselves in order to let God lead us to victory. One day when His kingdom is fully revealed, we will escape even the *presence* of sin. I for one cannot wait! But until that blessed time comes, we must lean on Him every day—and at frequent points throughout the day—in order to escape the *power* of sin. We waste our time when we fight temptation with only our higher goals and our loftier reforms, for God alone can give us strength to overcome our shortcomings. Here's how David put it:

> He delivered me from my strong enemy,
> And from those who hated me, for they were too mighty for me.
> They confronted me in the day of my calamity
> But the LORD was my stay. (Ps. 18:17–18)

Help Me, Lord!

Look at both halves of this imperative petition, for it takes both to understand the full-service help the Lord provides.

When we pray for protection from temptation, we are asking God to spare us from exposure to situations that would severely test our vulnerability. He has said that He will never allow us to be tempted beyond what we are able to bear (1 Cor. 10:13). What a promise! Our Father has already measured the difficulty levels on all the temptations we're going to face, and none of them are able to defeat us unless we decide to let them. Even if we find ourselves in a difficult situation—where sinning would be so easy and finding someone to understand would be no problem—*we can pray to be delivered from yielding to the temptation* and building another mountain of debt between us and our heavenly Father.

As you start your day, ask God to keep you as far away from compromising situations as possible—the copy machine gossip, the lottery tickets, the wicked Web sites—wherever you're liable to lose sight of the kingdom. And as you pray throughout the day, ask Him for the strength to keep you from searching these places out yourself, especially when you're tired or discouraged, when you've unwittingly let your guard down. You know the sins that cause you the most trouble. You know the warning lights that flash when you're in the wrong place, around the wrong people, or under the influence of the wrong motive. Instead of letting them become stumbling blocks, make each one a trigger that reminds you to pray—not to grit your teeth, not to fight—to trust that "greater is He who is in you than he who is in the world" (1 John 4:4).

When your hope for personal holiness is in Jesus Christ alone, you'll find you have muscles you never knew you had.

Need Anything Else?

Remember the story of Jesus' temptation? In one of the most dramatic events in all the Bible, the devil met Him one-on-one in the wilderness—pure evil and pure righteousness squaring off for supremacy.

First, he made an appeal to His body. With Jesus physically starved from nearly a month and a half of fasting, the devil tempted Him with a taste of bread.

Second, he made an appeal to His soul. High on top of the temple, with a mass of potential followers milling below, ready to swarm to the spectacle of a miracle-working Messiah, the devil made a power play for His pride.

Third, he made an appeal to His spirit. Up a notch from the temple to the mountaintops, the devil offered Him all the kingdoms in all the world . . . if He would merely bow down and worship him.

But the Father supplied the Son with everything He needed—*body, soul, and spirit*—to withstand the onslaught of Satan's lies and deception.

And today God offers us—His children—the same provision.

- It covers our *past*—forgiveness for every sin we've ever committed.
- It covers our *present*—our daily need for daily bread.
- It covers our *future*—deliverance from each coming temptation.

We can live this day worry-free and with a clean conscience because our Father has us covered all the way around.

5

FEEL THE POWER

Praying without ceasing shouldn't have an ending, and it doesn't. But Jesus closes the Lord's Prayer—our pattern for kingdom praying—with a benediction that again reveals a God-focused frame of mind, an eternal perspective that should run through all our prayers, all the time.

> "For Yours is the kingdom and the power and the glory forever. Amen." (Matt. 6:13b)

Oh, how quickly it rolls off our lips, how easy it is to withdraw from our memory banks. But encapsulated in this sacred sentence are all the confidence, assurance, and understanding you'll ever need in order to walk into your next meeting or appointment with your head up, to face the results of your latest lab work or job application, to walk through a difficult situation with your teenager, or to confront your spouse about a long-standing matter of concern.

Never fear: The kingdom will come.

His power will prevail.

He will cause His glory to shine.

All you have to do is trust Him. This Father who loves you beyond your ability to grasp it also has divine authority beyond life's ability to defeat you.

When you wrap your prayers in awe and worship—concentrating on the *who* instead of the *whats, wheres, whys,* and *whens*—He rewards you with the knowledge that you are in the presence of complete provision.

Praise the Lord!

POINT OF ORDER

Many times, however, we quote this final passage from the Lord's Prayer in almost a singsong fashion. Not that there's a right or wrong way to say it, but let me make one suggestion that may help you break the cycle of rote memorization and force you to think about what you're praying.

Place the emphasis on the word *Your.* Or for the more traditional among us, *Thine.*

We've been discovering through this entire book that the focus of prayer is always supposed to be on God, always looking upward, outward, forward. We've also seen that we humans are prone to worry more about *our* kingdoms, place undue trust in *our own* power, gravitate toward situations and positions where *we* get the glory.

Therefore, we need the discipline of making sure that we remember whose kingdom matters. We need the realization that we can do nothing by ourselves but that His power can turn any event toward His will and draw any person to repentance and salvation. We need a constant check on our own pride and self-importance—a daily desire to do all things for His praise and glory.

Yours is the kingdom.

Yours is the power.

Yours is the glory.

Now and forever. Amen and amen.

So as we keep coming back to this line from the Lord's Prayer throughout the day, we remind ourselves always to look beyond the visible, the obvious, the natural, the immediate. We focus on this One "who made the world and all things in it," who is not "served by human hands, as though He needed anything, since He Himself gives to all people life and breath and all things" (Acts 17:24–25).

When God fills up our scope of vision, we can't help but see things in a heavenly light.

Yours Is the Kingdom

The first part of this benediction reminds us that our greatest desire and privilege as children of God is to participate in the work of His kingdom. He is the King, and we gladly serve Him. He alone can grant us the resources we need for daily, victorious living. Therefore, all the commitments and requests we make in prayer are placed in the context of the higher purposes of God, the surpassing wisdom of His will, the mighty, flowing river of His eternal kingdom.

And, as we saw before, this kingdom-focused living offers you an added bonus. When the driving desire of your life is to seek the advancement of His kingdom in the world that lies right in front of you—your home, your school, your workplace, even your weekly trip to the grocery—He removes all your reasons for worrying about the things you need. How foolish to "store up for yourselves treasures on earth, where moth and rust destroy, and where thieves break in and steal." With God acknowledged as your total source of supply, you can "store up for yourselves treasures in heaven, where neither moth nor rust destroys, and where thieves do not break in and steal; for where your treasure is, there your heart will be also" (Matt. 6:19–21).

> Be anxious for nothing, but in everything by prayer and supplication with thanksgiving let your requests be made known to God. And the peace of God, which surpasses all comprehension, will guard your hearts and your minds in Christ Jesus. (Phil. 4:6–7)

Yesterday's prayer was for yesterday's needs. And tomorrow you'll need to recommit yourself to pursuing kingdom purposes. But for now there's just today—and a God more than able not only to meet your needs but also to enable you to meet His desires.

The kingdom comes first. The kingdom comes last. *The kingdom comes . . .* throughout the day.

Yours Is the Power

On September 15, 2000, our seminary community was shaken by the slaughter of seven young people at Wedgewood Baptist Church in Fort Worth, Texas. You probably remember the tragic event. Larry Ashcroft, a deluded outcast with contempt for all things religious, burst into a Wednesday night youth concert and ruthlessly, randomly gunned down seven church members. Three of the young adults killed included two students and a recent alumnus of our institution. Two other seminary students were seriously injured.

I remember the Lord bringing this passage to mind during those horrific few days of maddening questions and boiling disbelief:

> But we have this treasure in earthen vessels, so that the surpassing greatness of the power will be of God and not from ourselves; we are afflicted in every way, but not crushed; perplexed, but not despairing; persecuted, but not forsaken; struck down, but not destroyed; always carrying about in the body the dying of Jesus, so that the life of Jesus also

> may be manifested in our body. For we who
> live are constantly being delivered over to
> death for Jesus' sake, so that the life of Jesus
> also may be manifested in our mortal flesh.
> (2 Cor. 4:7–11)

If ever there were a time when all of us felt totally powerless in ourselves to help these families deal with their crushing losses, this was it. If ever there were a time when innocent people felt powerless to defend themselves and their friends from the hellish rain of a wretched gunman's bullets, it was that mournful late summer evening at the corner of Whitman and Walton Streets.

But these verses make clear that there is power beyond the lashing anger of human hate. What life can dish out, God can transform into a spectacle of His glory, for *His* is the power. *All* power. *The* power. In the words of one of the ministers who prayed during the emotional memorial service following the Wedgewood tragedy, "We thank you, God, that you waste nothing."

And even on our more ordinary days, when we feel powerless to deal with a back-biting coworker, or to accomplish the mountain of tasks that lie between now and bedtime, or to make sense of an unfulfilling life that seems to be going nowhere, we can quit trying to respond in our own strength and rely instead on God's power.

Most of the struggles we have over daily provision, forgiveness, and temptation to sin—the three requests from the previous chapter that encircle every need in the human life—are the result of continuing to labor under the mistaken idea that we can live the Christian life out of our own resources. We must understand that we are spiritually *impotent,* but He is *omnipotent.*

We are without hope, but He is without limits.

We are weak, but He is strong.

New Testament scholars have coined a phrase to capture this wonderful truth that we can experience God's eternal power in the present day. They call it "eschatology becoming actualized"—*eschatalogy* being a reference to final realities. When we declare "thine is the power," we are praising God for allowing us to experience in actual, real time the power of God that will last for all time.

Perhaps this benediction brings into sharper focus some of the great promises of Scripture, such as:

> I can do all things through Him who strengthens me. . . . And my God shall supply all your needs according to His riches in glory in Christ Jesus. (Phil. 4:13, 19)

As you read these familiar verses again, can't you just hear the echoing refrain? "Thine is the power." No matter what you're experiencing in your daily life, be confident that all power belongs to your King, and His power is available to you as you seek His kingdom.

YOURS IS THE GLORY

Glory is a great Bible word. It refers to God's presence being made manifest on earth. In Old Testament times

God's glory was seen in such spectacular expressions as the burning bush, the pillar of fire that guided the Hebrews by night, and the delivery of the Ten Commandments to Moses on Mount Sinai.

In the New Testament, of course, God is glorified through His Son, Jesus Christ—"glory as of the only begotten from the Father, full of grace and truth" (John 1:14). When He turned the water into wine at the wedding feast in Cana, we are told that this miracle "manifested His glory" (John 2:11). His raising of Lazarus from the dead was intended "for the glory of God, so that the Son of God may be glorified by it" (John 11:4). And on the Mount of Transfiguration, His face, His hair, even the clothes on His back radiated with a glimpse of heavenly splendor that flung three tough, weather-worn disciples face down, flat on the ground, terrified at the awesome display of His holiness.

Such glory catches your breath, sends shivers up your spine, awakens you to realities uncommonly seen by eyes grown dim in this dingy, moth-eaten world. But nowhere was His glory more evident than when He approached the cross, praying in selfless abandon:

> "I glorified You on the earth, having accomplished the work which You have given Me to do. Now, Father, glorify Me together with Yourself, with the glory which I had with You before the world was." (John 17:4–5)

He had done it all perfectly, just as His Father had told Him. He was within hours of completing His redemptive mission by shedding His blood for the sins of the world. Yet He had the vision to look beyond the splintery cross, the piercing nails, the heaving gasps for breath, out across the centuries to those He was sending into human history, just as His Father had sent Him into the world.

> "The glory which You have given Me I have given to them, that they may be one, just as We are one. . . . Father, I desire that they also, whom You have given Me, be with Me where I am, so that they may see My glory which You have given Me, for You loved Me before the foundation of the world." (John 17:22, 24)

For those who are in a saving relationship with Jesus Christ, there is something breathless even about daily, ordinary living, for "these whom He called, He also justified; and these whom He justified, He also glorified" (Rom. 8:30). The Scriptures tell us that in heaven "the city has no need for the sun or of the moon to shine on it, for the glory of God has illumined it, and its lamp is the Lamb" (Rev. 21:23). Yet somehow, even here where pollutants contaminate our drinking water, industrial exhaust thickens the air, and seasonal allergens drive us to the medicine cabinet for relief, we can experience the glory of God "on earth as it is in heaven."

When we acknowledge "Thine is the glory," we dare request in childlike faith that He reveal His glory in and through us. What a wonder that Almighty God would choose to express His awesome presence through our actions and deeds, lighting the corners of a world that is growing increasingly dark and spiritually bankrupt.

Where God's people are, God's glory shines. The curtain that stands between earth and eternity parts for just a moment. And those smothering under the oppressive, suffocating deception of sin and its nasty side effects can open wide their weary arms and bathe in its liberating light.

Will you be an outpost of glory in your corner of the world? Then seek His kingdom, make your life a pure, available instrument for His power, and be willing to invade the darkness around you with anything He tells you to do and anything He tells you to say.

Glory be to God!

FINALLY

I hope that God will place this pattern of prayer into your heart and life. I hope you will pray it every morning and keep it on your mind throughout the day. God has done something marvelous in my heart by teaching me to use His prayer in this way, and I know He will do the same—and even greater—in your own life.

Today, when I walk around the seminary campus, I am constantly thinking, "Lord, your name is at stake here." When I respond to people who sometimes misunderstand or misuse me, I don't take it personally or try to defend myself. I just say, "Lord, the only issue I care about is this:

Is your name being exalted in this decision I'm making, in this action I'm proposing, in this thing I'm about to do? If not, my mind is changed right now. But if so, I'll stand against any opposition in order to declare the name of the Lord." Not too many years from now, the name Hemphill may not mean a lot, but the name of the Lord Jesus Christ will stand forever. And I want to make His name hallowed in and through my life.

When I wake up in the morning, I consider that whatever I will do for the kingdom is the most important business in front of me today. It may be something obvious or expected in my routine. But even during those times when I'm outside my official capacities or my church experience, I'm still seeking the kingdom because I know it can invade my life at any place, at any moment. Even the most mundane moments in my life have become electrified with meaning as God has shown me the kingdom realities that dwell within them.

When I consider the will of God for this day, I have decided that my answer is yes—no matter what the question is. Too many times I've waited to hear the question before I decided what I would answer. But as a Christian, I know that the only answer I can give to my Father is "yes, Lord." *Do you want me to serve you overseas?* The answer's yes. *Do you want me to share the gospel with my next-door neighbor?* The answer's yes. *Do you want me to go back to the person I spoke to harshly or apologize to the person I'm upset with?* Yes, yes, the answer's yes. I don't know what the question is; I don't even *care* what the question is. My answer is "yes, Lord, yes."

My prayer is that you will join me in making each moment a kingdom experience. We are here on assignment, and we've been given our orders. Let us pray that God will help us spend every minute in His presence and glorify His name with every inch of our being.

Why not start right now: *"Our Father who is in heaven . . ."*

PRAYER SUGGESTIONS

I have sought to provide several suggestions that might offer further guidance as you incorporate the Prayer of Jesus into your daily spiritual life. These suggestions are not intended to be exhaustive, but rather instructive. Allow the Holy Spirit to bring fresh ideas and insights to your mind each day as you follow Jesus' pattern of prayer.

Our

1. Focus on the privilege implicit in being allowed to join Jesus in addressing God as Father.
2. Thank Him for providing for your salvation.
3. Remember the larger context of the community of faith as you pray. Your relationship to Christ connects you to believers around the world, and this should be reflected in every aspect of your prayer life.

Father

1. Focus on the intimacy embodied in the parent/child relationship.
2. Remember that your heavenly Father is perfectly good and fully capable of meeting your every need (see Matt. 7:7–12 and Luke 11:9–13).
3. Talk to God with the same honesty and intimacy you would if you were talking to a "perfect" earthly father.

Who art in heaven

1. Focus on God's sovereign ability to provide for your daily needs (John 14:12–21).

2. Remember that your heavenly Father owns the cattle on a thousand hills; in other words, all resources are available to Him.

3. Renew your commitment to love and obey Him as both your loving Father and as Lord of the universe.

Hallowed be Thy name

1. Begin this section of praying by praising God's name. The Psalms will greatly assist you in your praise time. I have included a few partial references to get you started. Read them in their context, and use them in your prayer time.

- Psalm 5:11: "Those who love Thy name may exult in thee."
- Psalm 8:1: "O LORD, our Lord, How majestic is Thy name in all the earth."
- Psalm 66:1–2: "Shout joyfully to God, all the earth; sing the glory of His name."

2. The second aspect of praying *Hallowed be Thy name* is the commitment to honor God's name through your speech, actions, and behavior throughout the day. Ask the Lord to make you ever mindful that you bear His name and to strengthen you to bring honor to His name.

Thy Kingdom come

1. Focus on the privilege God has given you to share in His kingdom.

2. Ask Him to make you sensitive to opportunities to spread His kingdom through word and deed.

3. Ask Him to make you aware that every moment of every day is a kingdom-infused moment.

4. Pray for all those who are involved in kingdom work throughout your community and around the world.

Thy will be done

1. Focus on God's will for your life as revealed in His Word. "I delight to do Thy will, O my God; Thy law is within my heart" (Ps. 40:8).

2. Ask God to make you sensitive to His guidance moment by moment.

3. Tell Him that the answer is *yes* to any request He might make.

Give us this day our daily bread

1. Remember that the "us" in this phrase provides us with the privilege of praying for the needs of others. You should start a prayer journal with various requests and keep a record of God's responses.

2. Lay out your petitions for food, shelter, and clothing. You can tell your Father about all your needs; after all, He is *your* Father. Ask Him to show you how His answers to your request will better enable you to serve His kingdom.

2. Remember that prayer is focused on the Father's kingdom, not yours. When you focus on His kingdom, it reduces anxiety and reminds you that He is providing for your kingdom.

And forgive us our debts, as we also have forgiven our debtors

1. Be specific as you pray about the sin issues that could keep you from enjoying fellowship with the Father.

2. Claim the promise of 1 John 1:9: "If we confess our sins, He is faithful and righteous to forgive our sins and to cleanse us from all unrighteousness."

3. Ask the Father to remind you of any debts you have failed to forgive in others. He will grant you the strength to give those indebted to you the release that you desire as you ask for personal forgiveness.

Do not lead us into temptation, but deliver us from evil

1. Ask the Father to guide every step you take today. By nature, God who is wholly righteous cannot lead you into evil. Declare your intention to follow Him.

2. Ask for and accept the strength to turn from temptation and evil.

3. Pray for other Christians you know who may be facing temptation to evil. Remember to pray for those facing persecution.

For Thine is the kingdom, and the power, and the glory, forever. Amen.

1. Ask the Father to make you sensitive to the truth of these affirmations. When you pray and act upon the assurance that these are absolute truths, you will have full confidence that your prayer has been heard and will be rewarded.

Hints for Using The Prayer of Jesus *in the Church and Small Groups*

1. Obtain a copy of *The Prayer of Jesus* for all participants.
2. Study the material together and discuss the implications of each section. Some churches will prefer to study the material over a period of several weeks while others may prefer an intensive retreat setting.
3. Choose a prayer partner or two and meet together on a regular basis for prayer based on the Jesus pattern.
4. When you meet for prayer, you should also establish a time for "kingdom accountability." Ask each other the following seven questions on a regular basis.

- What did you do today (this week) that "hallowed God's name"?
- What actions, words, or deeds brought reproach on His name? (Discuss how you might make amends.)
- What kingdom opportunity did you encounter, and how did you respond?
- How have you responded to God's will today? (Share the victories of obedience, and seek forgiveness for issues of disobedience.)
- How have you experienced God's daily provision?
- How is your spiritual debt ledger? (What do you need forgiveness for, and who do you need to forgive? What practical actions are you prepared to take?)
- Have you avoided all issues of temptation and experienced spiritual victory?

Let's think a moment about how God might use this accountability time. As you use these questions for confidential accountability, you can pray *together* about needs and opportunities that each of you face. For example, perhaps you are forced to answer the question 6 with the response that you lost your temper and spoke angrily to a colleague at work. You become aware that your angry response profaned God's name and thus hurt your witness to this unsaved friend. As you discuss this situation, the Holy Spirit prompts you to ask the colleague for forgiveness for your curt response. Your prayer partners join you in praying for the strength to seek forgiveness, and they commit to hold you accountable for that response to God at the next meeting.

Who knows—when you ask for forgiveness for your angry words, you may open the door for a witnessing opportunity. Your colleague may be so surprised by your apology that he/she may ask you why you would apologize for such a trivial issue. You could then explain that your commitment to Christ makes you aware that you bear His name. I truly believe that such kingdom-focused praying and responding has the power to transform churches, communities, and nations.

I would love to hear the many stories of God's incredible provision for you and your church as you seek first the kingdom of God.

THE NAMES OF GOD

You may find it helpful to focus on specific names (titles) revealed by God throughout Scripture. These names were given by God to help us understand His character. You may not use each name daily, but as you come to understand the significance of each one, you will use the appropriate name as the Spirit prompts you.

Elohim (Powerful God)

God is the creator of all that exists and stands alone as eternal God. This name should give you confidence as you pray.

Adonai (Lord)

He is Lord or master of the universe. You can know that He is sufficient, and thus you can freely surrender your life and your day to Him as your Lord.

El Elyon (God Most High)

He is the possessor of the heavens and the earth. He alone can provide for our needs.

El Shaddai (Almighty God)

This name reminds us that we can accomplish nothing

in our own strength, but that He has abundant resources to enable us to do all that He requires.

Jehovah (I Am)

God is absolutely self-existent. He is the same yesterday, today, and forever. He is faithful to fulfill His promises.

Jehovah Jireh (The Lord Provides)

God can be trusted with your most precious gift. You must surrender your "Isaac" (most valued possession) in order to experience the release of God's blessing. Ask God to show Himself as "Provider."

Jehovah Rophe (The Lord Heals)

Our circumstances never test God; they only test us. When you need physical, emotional, or spiritual healing, look to Him.

Jehovah Nissi (The Lord Is My Banner)

The Lord is a banner of victory. Look to Him for victory over sin and temptation.

Jehovah Mekadesh (The Lord Who Sanctifies You)

As you pray this name, ask God to keep you from sin and to allow you to be used to serve Him today.

Jehovah Shalom (The Lord Is Peace)

When you are feeling agitated and insufficient, you can call upon the Lord who is Peace.

Jehovah Tsidkenu (The Lord Is Our Righteousness)

God by nature is righteous, and therefore we commit to live by His righteous standards. The good news is that He desires to be our righteousness as we pray for deliverance from evil.

Jehovah Rohi (The Lord Is My Shepherd)

Memorize the twenty-third Psalm, and pray various parts of it as the Holy Spirit brings it to mind.

Jehovah Shammah (The Lord Is There)

When you feel alone and need to sense His presence, call upon Him as Jehovah Shammah.

I discuss the context and significance of each of these names in my companion book, *The Names of God*. I encourage you to read *The Names of God* and incorporate God's name in your prayers as you declare it to be hallowed in your life.

ENDNOTES

Chapter 2

1. These findings come from Joachim Jeremias, tr. John Reumann, *The Lord's Prayer* (Philadelphia: Fortress Press, 1964), 2–5.

2. Jesus' prayer from the cross, "My God, My God, why hast thou forsaken me," does not begin with a reference to the Father because Jesus was quoting directly from an Old Testament source.

3. Corrie Ten Boom and John and Elizabeth Sherrill, *The Hiding Place* (New York: Bantam Books, 1971), 197.

Chapter 3

1. If you desire to witness but have never found a method that works well in the marketplace, I would recommend a new tool called *GotLife*. It is simple but complete and comes with a comprehensive training CD. You can find the Action G.E.A.R. in your Christian bookstore, or you can order by calling 800-856-8886 or by logging on to www.gotlife.org.